SEASON SIX

GROWING IN YOUR MISSION

Carl Simmons

Group
Loveland, Colorado
group.com

Group resources actually work!

This Group resource incorporates our R.E.A.L. approach to ministry. It reinforces a growing friendship with Jesus, encourages long-term learning, and results in life transformation, because it's

Relational
Learner-to-learner interaction enhances learning and builds Christian friendships.

Experiential
What learners experience through discussion and action sticks with them up to 9 times longer than what they simply hear or read.

Applicable
The aim of Christian education is to equip learners to be both hearers and doers of God's Word.

Learner-based
Learners understand and retain more when the learning process takes into consideration how they learn best.

SEASON SIX

Growing Out: From Disciples to Disciplers

GROWING IN YOUR MISSION

Visit our website: **group.com**

Credits
Editor: Lee Sparks
Editorial Director: Rebecca L. Manni
Chief Creative Officer: Joani Schultz
Assistant Editor: Alison Imbriaco
Art Director: Paul Povolni
Book Designer: Jean Bruns
Cover Designer: Holly Voget
Illustrator: Wes Comer
Print Production: Paragon Prepress
Production Manager: Peggy Naylor

ISBN 978-0-7644-4007-6

10 9 8 7 6 5 4 3 2 1 19 18 17 16 15 14 13 12 11 10

Printed in the United States of America.

Contents

What Growing Out Looks Like

Growing Out is more than a series of Bible studies—it's a progression that will take you and your group from becoming disciples of Jesus to becoming discipl*ers* of *others* in Jesus. As you move through each season, you'll grow from the inside out—and as you grow, your life in Jesus will naturally expand and branch out to others in your world.

And here's the best part: As you grow out together, you'll realize how much you're *already* discipling others—starting with those in your group!

Growing Out is designed to allow you to jump in at the most appropriate place for you and your group. To help you discover your entry point, take a look at these descriptions of each season:

Season One: Growing in Jesus focuses on developing your relationship with Jesus. Because, let's face it, the first person you have to disciple is *yourself.* More to the point, you need to learn how to let Jesus *show* you how to be his disciple. So in this season, we focus on your relationship with Jesus and how to deepen it through spiritual disciplines such as prayer, worship, Bible study…and, not least of all, through your relationships with other Christians (such as the ones you're sitting with).

After you've been grounded in your relationship with Jesus, how does that shine into the rest of your life? That's where *Season Two: Growing in Character* comes in. This season focuses on how you can invite Jesus into your most important relationships—with your family, your friends, and the people you work with—and how to keep Jesus at the center of all of them.

Season Three: Growing in Your Gifts focuses on discovering the gifts, talents, and passions God has given you and how God might want to use them to serve others—whether that's inside or outside your church walls. After this season, you'll have a better sense of who God has created you to be, and why.

And with that, you're ready for *Season Four: Growing Others.* If you've gotten this far, you've developed and deepened your walk with Jesus, you've learned how to actually live it out among those people you most care about, and you've begun to discover how God has uniquely built you. Now...how do you take what God has shown you and help *others* walk through the same process?

If you've completed Seasons One through Three, you already know the answer because that's *exactly* what you've been doing with your group. Season Four will help you reach out to even more people. Call it mentoring, discipling, or just being a good Christian friend to someone who needs it, after Season Four, you'll be ready to come alongside anyone who's ready to have a deeper relationship with Jesus. Just like you in Season One.

In the final two seasons, you'll explore what it takes to lead others where God wants you *and* them to go next. Because as you've walked through the first four seasons, guess what? You've been growing. Others know it. And God is honoring it. So whether you see yourself that way or not, God has matured you to the point where you're ready to lead. And we're going to help you get *more* ready.

Season Five: Growing in Leadership focuses on how to stay functional even as you learn how to lead. You'll walk together through the foibles of leadership—communication, conflict resolution, building consensus, learning how to adjust your ministry, and learning to stay focused on God instead of "*your* ministry."

And as you keep growing out, God may well put things on your heart that you'll need to be the one to initiate. That brings us, at last, to *Season 6: Growing in Your Mission.* God has given you a specific vision for ministry, and now you literally need to make the dream real. We'll help walk you through the issues that come with a God-given vision. Issues like, first of all, how do you know it really *is* God, and not just you? How do you get others on board (and praying—a *lot*)? And how will *you* keep growing, even as the vision continues to grow and take shape?

Because, no matter where you are, you never stop *growing out*. God will always see to that.

Enjoy Growing Out, and may God bless you as you grow out together!

Why R.E.A.L. Discipleship Works

Before we go any further, go back and take one more look at the copyright page of this book (it's page 2—the one with all the credits). Go to the top of the page where it declares, "Group resources actually work!" Take a minute or two to read that entire section describing Group's R.E.A.L. guarantee, and then come back to this introduction. I'll wait for you here…

Now that we're literally back on the same page, let's explore R.E.A.L. a little more deeply. Your desire to go deeper is the reason you're reading this book, and it's not only our goal but also our *passion* to help you accomplish that desire. When it comes right down to it, there's nothing more R.E.A.L. than discipleship. Think about it:

Relational

At the heart of it, discipleship *is* relationship. First and foremost, it's about developing the most important relationship you'll ever have—your relationship with Jesus. And as your relationship with Jesus grows, it becomes far more than anything you've ever imagined.

Like any great relationship, it doesn't develop on its own. It's intentional. It's work. But it's way more than that. What we get back is far more than what we put in. How could it *not* be? It's a relationship with *Jesus*. And as that relationship grows, we'll want to bring Jesus into every other relationship we have.

So we've kept that in mind as we've designed these sessions. You'll gain a deeper understanding of God's Word, but even more important, you'll discover how to share what you've learned with those around you. And that discovery *has* to happen in community. We've made these sessions very relational because, after all, you're learning how to become discipl*ers*. By definition, that means learning how to speak God into others' lives. As you do that, you'll get as much back as you give, if not more. Because that's what happens in great relationships.

You'll notice that we often suggest getting into pairs or smaller groups. That's because participation—and learning, not to mention life change—increases when everyone's involved. It's more challenging, sure, but it's also more rewarding. Be sure to take advantage of the times we suggest it.

All this is a long way of saying that by the time you've finished this season, not only will you have a deeper relationship with Jesus, but your spiritual relationships with others will be richer and deeper than you had ever anticipated. And when that happens, be sure to thank us; a little affirmation goes a long way toward helping us to keep doing what we do here.

Experiential

Experiences? Yeah, we've got experiences. And as you discover together where God wants to take you next, you'll have experiences of your own long after you've completed these sessions.

Research has proven again and again that the more senses we engage in the learning process, the more likely a session is to stick and truly become woven into our daily lives. Jesus knew that, too. That's why he used everyday items to make his message more real. Not only that, but he invited people out of their comfort zones to conquer their fear of the unknown. We like to do that, too. A lot.

And because it's so different from what we're used to when studying God's Word, this is often the hardest part of R.E.A.L. learning for people to embrace. Is it *really* OK to have fun when we're studying the Bible? Does it truly honor God? Wouldn't it distract us from focusing on God?

First, let's make it clear that these are legitimate concerns. I've wrestled with all of them as I've developed these sessions. We want to honor Jesus. Discipleship isn't a joke. It's serious business. It's about the rest of your life and how you'll glorify God with it. There's nothing more serious than that.

Nonetheless, sometimes the best way to get serious is to set aside our expectations first, so we're able to open up and get down to what we're *really* wrestling with, rather than just come up with the right answers, go home, and never really deal with the things God wants us to deal with. The experiences in this book go a long way toward

accomplishing that. Here are just a few of the ways people "got R.E.A.L." as we field-tested this curriculum:

- A church elder in our group declared from the beginning, in no uncertain terms and with a bit of a growl, "I don't *do* games." A few weeks in, he shared, "This is exactly what [my wife and I] needed right now." Several weeks later, this same game-hating elder proclaimed, "I really *liked* that activity! It worked *perfectly*!"
- One of our hosts, who also prepared the session's snack, suggested, "I'll make sure I pull it out of the oven just when everyone gets here." She understood that not only the look and taste of the snack but also the smell would help people experience the session more acutely.
- A pastor in our group enjoyed one particular activity so much that he went ahead and used it in his own church's small-group training class.
- Another woman shared how her husband had been initially skeptical about R.E.A.L. learning, and about small groups in general. (Anyone else detecting a pattern among the men, by the way?) Several sessions later, she was positively glowing as she shared how we'd "broken through" and how much he'd opened up as we'd gone along—and for that matter, how he was still talking about the session the next morning.

Discipleship *is* a lifelong adventure. And we're here to help you embrace that adventure. Together. That's why we've not only built in activities to get you thinking about your faith (and expressing it) in brand-new ways, but...well, let's just move on to...

Applicable

This is pretty straightforward. You're here not only to learn but also to grow. And that means taking what you've learned and using it.

We give you opportunities in every session to do that—to give you a safe place to experiment, if you will. We also provide opportunities at the end of each session for you to take what you've learned and Walk It Out in the rest of your life—so that your faith *becomes* your life, and you can take practical steps toward sharing your life in Jesus so others can see and respond to it as well.

Learner-Based

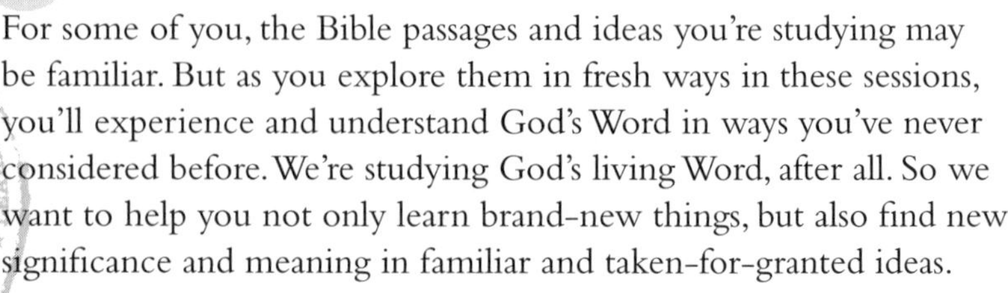

For some of you, the Bible passages and ideas you're studying may be familiar. But as you explore them in fresh ways in these sessions, you'll experience and understand God's Word in ways you've never considered before. We're studying God's living Word, after all. So we want to help you not only learn brand-new things, but also find new significance and meaning in familiar and taken-for-granted ideas.

Therefore, we've been very deliberate about choosing the right approaches for the right sessions. When an activity works, let's get up and do it. If a movie clip brings out the meaning of what you're learning, throw in the DVD and let's talk. If a snack works not only as an icebreaker but also as a discussion starter about a much deeper subject, let's serve it up and dig in. And when it's time to just open up God's Word and really wrap our minds around what God wants us to understand about a given subject—or to be reminded of what God has already shown us (because we forget that all too easily, too)—then we'll bust out our Bibles and read as many passages as it takes to begin to grasp (or re-grasp) that.

You're also here to discover who *you* are in Jesus. The body of Christ is made of millions of unique parts. You're one of them. We *know* one size doesn't fit all, and we've built Growing Out to reflect that. So whatever reaches you best—the Bible study, the activities, the questions, the take-home pieces, whatever—use them to their fullest extent. I'll give you some more ideas of how to do this in the next two sections.

However you approach these sessions—and whether you do that as a leader or as a participant—be sure to help others in your group approach things in the ways God can best reach them. And as God works in all of you, celebrate it. A lot.

May God bless you as you begin your journey together. And as God takes each of you to the places and experiences he has prepared for you, never forget: You're all in this together. You, God, and everyone he puts in your path. And *that's* discipleship.

—*Carl Simmons*

About the Sessions

Now that you know why we do what we do, let's talk about *how* we do it—and more important—how *you* can do it.

You may already understand this, but just so we're clear: Discipleship is *not* about completing a curriculum. It's about developing and deepening the most important spiritual relationships you have—first with God and then with those God brings you in contact with—because *none* of those relationships is an accident. They're all intentional, and we need to be intentional as well.

In fact, that's why we refer to each study as a season, rather than as a study, book, or quarter. Each of us grows at our own pace. Your season of growth might be longer or shorter than someone else's, and that's OK. God will take as long as you need to get you where he wants you. So spend as much time in each season as you need to. But stay committed to moving forward.

Also, each season has been built so that whether you're a participant or a leader, you can get the most out of each session. And that starts with the layout of each lesson. Keep a finger here, flip over to one of the sessions, and let's look at why this is so different.

This isn't just a leader guide. It's not just a guide for group members. It's *both*! And the way we've set up the sessions reflects that.

Leaders: The left-hand pages contain *your* instructions, so you're constantly on track and know what's happening next. What you do, what you say—all the basics are there. You'll also want to be sure to check out the Leader Notes beginning on page 147—they'll give you specific prep instructions for each session, as well as great tips to make each session the best it can be.

Group Members: You don't care about all that leader stuff, do you? Didn't think so. Now you don't need to. The right-hand pages are just for you. Write your answers, journal whatever else God is saying to you, record insights from your group discussions, doodle while you listen—you've got plenty of room for all of it. All the questions and Bible passages you'll be using are right there. Use your pages to get the most out of what God's showing you each week.

Got all that? Good. Now let's talk about what each session looks like.

Come and See In this (usually) brief opening section, you'll take time to unwind and transition from wherever you're coming from—a hectic drive to church on a Sunday morning or the end of a busy day—into the theme of the session. You and your group might enjoy a snack or a movie clip together; maybe it'll be an activity; maybe you'll just talk with someone else. Then you'll be ready to dig in deep. And maybe—because you were too busy having such a good time doing it—you won't even realize that you've already gotten down to business.

Seek and Find This is the heart of each session, and usually the longest section. You'll spend roughly a half-hour digging into God's Word and discovering its meaning in a way you hadn't realized before. You think you understand these things now? Just *wait*. Through a variety of experiences and powerful questions that take a fresh look both at Scripture and at what's going on in your own head and heart, you'll discover how God's Word *really* applies to your life.

Go You'll move from understanding how what you've been studying applies to your life to considering ways to act on it. Again, through meaningful experiences and questions, you'll discover what you can do with what God has shown you through today's session. Which will take you directly into…

Walk It Out This is the take-home part of the session. Past seasons of Growing Out provided specific suggestions for applying the session's lesson in practical ways. If you've gotten this far, however, you don't *need* suggestions. You just need to figure out how what you're learning applies to what you're already doing. And the only person who can answer that is you.

So in Seasons Five and Six, Walk It Out is an open-ended proposition. With a partner or partners, choose a weekly challenge that applies to what God's telling you about your situation. And then be obedient. Share what God is showing you with your group so they can pray for you and encourage you.

There's one more section to tell you about. It appears at the very end. It's not even part of the session per se, but it could end up meaning a lot to you.

Go Deeper I can't emphasize this enough, so I'm repeating it: Discipleship is *not* about completing a curriculum. It's about developing and deepening the most important spiritual relationships you have—first with God, then with those God has brought you in contact with—because *none* of those relationships is an accident.

Therefore, it's possible you'll work through this season and think, "Before I go any further, I really need a deeper understanding of..." That's why I've provided a list of resources at the end of each session to help you do just that. At Group, we're not shy about recommending other publishers—and if a resource applies to more than one area of spiritual growth, we'll recommend it more than once. This isn't about selling Group products (although there's always much more dancing in the halls here when that happens). It's about your growing relationship with Jesus, and being willing to invite God into whatever you're still wrestling with.

And that painful thing you're feeling when you do that? That's called growth. But the good news is: We're in this together. So pull over whenever you need to! Or jump right into the next season. We're here for you either way.

Which brings us to a little reminder at the very end of each session: If there's an area in which you'd like to see *us* dig deeper and create more resources to help *you,* tell us! Write to us at Group Publishing, Inc., P.O. Box 481, Loveland, CO 80539; or contact us via e-mail at smallgroupministry.com. We'd love to hear what you're thinking. (Yes—*really*!)

Choose Your Environment

Growing Out works well in a variety of venues. We want to help you wherever you are. Don't be shy about trying any of them! Here are some additional ideas, depending on your venue.

Sunday School

First, you may have noticed that I've chosen the word *group* instead of *class* throughout. Not every group is a class, but every class is a group—because you're not here just to study and learn facts; you're also here to learn how to live out what you've learned. Together. As a group. We hope that becomes even truer as you work through these sessions.

We've constructed these sessions to run an hour at a brisk pace, but we understand the limitations a Sunday school program can put on the amount of time you spend on a session. So if a great question has started a great discussion, and you don't want to cut it off, feel free to trim back elsewhere as needed. For example, since many of the people in our field-test group were couples who could talk on the way home, we discovered that making Walk It Out a take-home instead of an in-class piece was one good way to buy back time without losing impact.

Try not to be one of those groups that say, "Great—we can skip that experience now!" Remember, the more senses and learning styles you engage, the more these sessions will stick. So play with these activities. Give yourself permission to fail—but go in expecting God to do the unexpected.

And if you don't have specific time limitations, read on.

Small Groups

If you need more than an hour for a session—and you're not tied to a clock or a calendar—take it! Again, taking the time to understand what God wants to tell your group is *way* more important than "covering the material" or staying within the one-hour or 13-week parameters. This happened repeatedly while field-testing—a great discussion ensued, people got down to things they were really wrestling with, and we decided we'd explore the session further the following week.

Learn to recognize rabbit trails—and get off them sooner rather than later—but don't short-circuit those occasions when the Holy Spirit is really working in people's lives. Those occasions will happen often in these sessions. If you're having a rich discussion and are really digging in, take an extra week and dig even deeper. Give the full meaning of the session time to sink in.

One-on-One Discipleship

Although this curriculum is designed for a larger group setting, we absolutely don't want to discourage you from using it in a more traditional, one-on-one discipleship setting. True, some of the activities might not work in a setting this small, and if that's the case, feel free to bypass them and go directly into the Bible passages and questions—there are plenty left to work with. The important thing is that you work together through the issues themselves, and at the pace you need to move forward.

But don't take this as an opportunity to entirely excuse yourselves from experiences—have a little fun together, and see what God does. Allow yourselves to be surprised.

Also—and it's probably obvious for this and the next scenario—all those recommendations we make to form smaller groups or twosomes? You can skip those and jump right into the discussion or activity.

Smaller Groups or Accountability Groups

One more thing: We don't want to discourage you from doing one-on-one discipleship, especially if you've already got a good thing going. There are some great and healthy mentoring relationships out there, and if you're already involved in one, keep at it! That said, research has shown repeatedly that learning can happen at a more accelerated rate—and more profoundly—in settings other than the traditional teacher-student relationship. So if you're just starting out, consider gathering in groups of three or four.

- It's an environment that allows everyone to learn from one another. While there's often still a clear leader, the playing field feels more level, and the conversations often become more open and honest.
- If one person leaves for any reason—and there are plenty of legitimate ones—the group or accountability relationship isn't finished. Everyone else presses forward. No one is left hanging.
- The dynamics of a group of three or four are simpler than those of larger groups. And a group of three or four can be the best of both worlds, offering the rich discussions of a large group and the intimacy and accountability of one-on-one relationships.
- Again, we're about creating discipl*ers*, and a smaller group allows growing disciplers to test-drive their own instructions, struggles, and transparency in an environment in which they can be both honestly critiqued and wholeheartedly encouraged. And when that happens, growth happens—for everyone.

If you'd like to delve deeper into this subject, Greg Ogden's *Transforming Discipleship* (InterVarsity) is a great resource to get you started, as are any number of materials from ChurchSmart Resources (churchsmart.com).

Whatever setting or environment you use for Growing Out, use it to its fullest. May God bless your efforts and those of the people with whom you share life!

Getting Connected

Pass your books around the room, and have people write their names, phone numbers, e-mail addresses, and birthdays in the spaces provided. Then make it a point to stay in touch during the week.

name	phone	e-mail	birthday

Permission to Dream Big

"*Whenever I pray, I make my requests for all of you with joy, for you have been my partners in spreading the Good News about Christ from the time you first heard it until now. And I am certain that God, who began the good work within you, will continue his work until it is finally finished on the day when Christ Jesus returns*" (PHILIPPIANS 1:4-6).

In this session, we'll journey...

from → **to**

opening ourselves to whatever possibilities God may present... → believing that when God gives a vision, God means to *fulfill* it.

Before gathering, make sure you have...

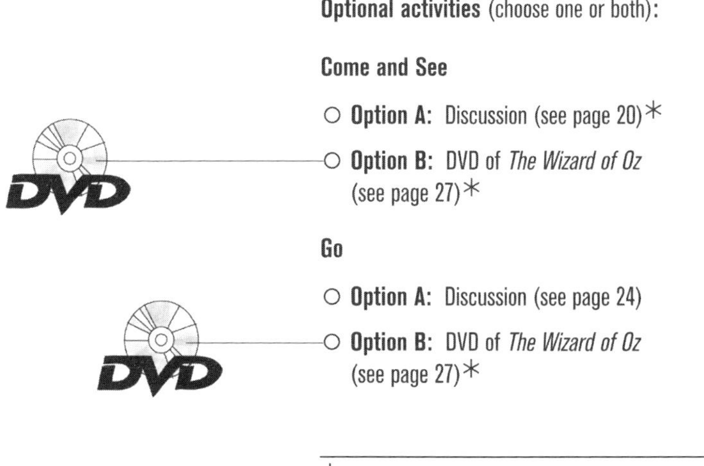

Optional activities (choose one or both):

Come and See

- ○ **Option A:** Discussion (see page 20)*
- ○ **Option B:** DVD of *The Wizard of Oz* (see page 27)*

Go

- ○ **Option A:** Discussion (see page 24)
- ○ **Option B:** DVD of *The Wizard of Oz* (see page 27)*

*See **Leader Notes,** page 149, for details.

Come and See

(about 10 minutes)

Leaders: Please note that the bolded sections of text are for you to read aloud. Feel free to change the wording to make yourself more comfortable. Or just use ours; that's why it's here.

» **Welcome! In this season, we'll explore what it takes to pursue a God-given vision—what pursuit of the vision looks like, how to help others see the vision, and what staying on the course God has set before us requires of us.**

Since you're here, we're going to assume a couple of things. One is that you're already sensing God calling you to something bigger. Whether you're the person in front or following someone else's lead, God's calling you (and others) to something brand new—or to tackle an existing ministry in a brand-new way. We'll begin exploring that today.

But first, here's the other assumption: You're trusting God's vision because God has *already* done something big in your lives. So before we move into what God has next for each of us, let's take a few minutes to reflect on some of the things God has done in our lives.

"*Vocation does not come from a voice 'out there' calling me to be something I am not. It comes from a voice 'in here' calling me to be the person I was born to be, to fulfill the original selfhood given to me at birth by God.*"

—Parker J. Palmer, Let Your Life Speak

If you chose **Option A**, *read on.*
If you're doing **Option B**, *go to page 27.*

» **Get into groups of four or five and discuss these questions:**

Come back together after 10 minutes. Share highlights and insights from your discussion.

◎ When has your understanding of who God is been radically changed? In other words, when did God reveal himself, his love, or his will to you in a brand-new way?

◎ Looking back now, how had God been preparing you even before that time?

›› The particular things that God has put on your hearts—or at least the idea that *it could really happen*—may be brand new, but I hope that the stories we've just shared have helped us see that God not only gives vision, but also gives the means to fulfill the vision he gives us. God is still deeply involved in our lives, and God wants us to be deeply involved in *his* life—and the lives of those around us.

So let's begin exploring what God might want to do with each of us.

Seek and Find

(about 30 minutes)

> *You need a certain dose of inspiration, a ray from on high, that is not in ourselves, in order to do beautiful things.*
>
> *—Vincent Van Gogh*

» **Over the course of this season, we'll look at a number of "case studies" from the Bible. We'll discover how others before us have handled walking out the vision God gave them, and then we'll examine how their examples might help us understand what God wants to do with the vision and mission he's given each of *us*.**

So let's look at our first example.

Ask for one or more volunteers to read Acts 10:9-35. Then discuss these questions:

» **Get back into the groups you formed earlier. Let another person from your group lead your next discussion.** (Pause.)

Earlier, you shared an example of God expanding your vision of who God is. This time, I'd like you to think of a more hands-on experience—something similar to what Peter experienced. In other words, think about a time God simultaneously fulfilled your expectations *and* blew those expectations out of the water. (Pause.)

> *Great faith, like great strength in general, is revealed by the ease of its workings. As 'the quality of mercy is not strained,' so also with faith. Most of what we think we see as the struggle of faith is really the struggle to act as if we had faith when in fact we do not.*
>
> *—Dallas Willard,* Hearing God

Take 10 minutes to discuss these questions in your groups:

Gather everyone's attention after 10 minutes, keeping people with their groups. Share highlights and insights from your discussion time.

» **Let's pull all this together now. There are, no doubt, some obvious answers to this next question—and it's OK to say them—but let's also push past the obvious as we discuss it.**

 **Acts 10:9-35**

◎ How would you describe Peter at the beginning of this passage? Why?

◎ How were the things Peter wanted for God similar to what God actually wanted? How were they different?

◎ How was Peter—and Peter's mission—changed by this encounter?

◎ What did God accomplish that wasn't just what *you* wanted to accomplish but what *God* wanted to accomplish?

◎ What limitations had you placed on the situation that God didn't have?

◎ How did that experience change you? How did it affect others around you?

◎ Why do we hold back when we're doing what we believe God wants us to do—since, after all, we believe it's *God's idea*?

Go

(about 20 minutes)

» **You've already shared examples of how God has grown you. Starting today, you'll have some new examples to observe—the group you're sitting with right now. For the rest of this season, you'll be working with this group and wrestling together with the things God is leading each of you into next. You're going to lead each other. You're going to learn from each other. And you're going to let God lead you, together.**

You've already talked today about times God has surprised you. So be prepared for God to surprise you even more this season, and be prepared to enjoy those surprises.

If you chose **Option A**, *read on.*
If you're doing **Option B**, *go to page 27.*

Ask for a volunteer to read Philippians 1:3-11.

» **You're here today because you feel God compelling you to take the next step in some way. Call it whatever you're comfortable calling it—conviction, a vision, a burden, a calling—but God's pushing you somehow, right now, to be someone more than who you've been so far. Now you'll get to talk about that specifically in your groups and begin to discover together what God might want to do.**

Turn back to your groups, and let someone else who hasn't led yet lead this piece. Discuss the questions, and then go on to the section called Walk It Out.

Let's come back together in 15 minutes.

Walk It Out

How does what you learned today apply to where you're at right now? How can you put it into practice? Take five minutes in your groups to write one thing you'll do this week to make today's lesson more real in your own life. Share your choices with your group, and make plans to connect before the next session to check in and encourage one another.

Philippians 1:3-11

◎ Describe as well as you can what God is leading you to do, or be a part of, right now. What do you think your role is?

◎ Put your own expectations or ambitions to the side for a moment. What *could* God do with this vision? Whether you believe it yet or not, say it aloud.

If Christ's redemptive work was, in part, intended to restore the image of God in us and if creativity is central to God's being, then creativity should become more and more a part of who we are.

—Robert Gelinas, **Finding the Groove: Composing a Jazz-Shaped Faith**

Because where God gives a vision, God gives what we need to fulfill it, I'll "Walk It Out" by

___

___

___

Go continued

Regain everyone's attention, keeping people with their groups. Reread Philippians 1:4-6, and then pray for all of your groups. Say something like,

prayer

» **Lord, we thank you for bringing us together and for the groups *you* have created here today. Just as we can only glimpse the vision you have for each of us, we can only guess what you might accomplish through each of these groups as you grow us closer together.**

Open our eyes to what you want to do as we work and learn together over the course of this season. Give us a deeper understanding of how you want to use us to make your presence more real to everyone you put in front of us. In Jesus' name, amen.

SEEING IT DIFFERENTLY

Come and See–Option B

LEADER *To prompt your group to think about a session in a fresh way, we'll occasionally recommend video clips that your group can enjoy in place of (or in addition to) another part of the session. You'll be surprised by how effectively movies can portray eternal truths, or at least point toward them.*

Instead of the opening group discussion, watch a scene from *The Wizard of Oz*. Cue the movie to 17:00 (DVD Chapter 10), as Dorothy shouts "Auntie Em!" Stop the clip at 21:37, after Dorothy says, "Now I…I *know* we're not in Kansas."

GROUP

◎ When has God had to knock you on the head so you could see things differently? What changed?

◎ Looking back now, how had God been preparing you even before that time?

Go–Option B

Instead of the original opening for Go, watch another scene from *The Wizard of Oz*. Advance the movie to 31:12 (DVD Chapter 18), as Dorothy says, "Oh, I'd give anything to get out of Oz altogether." Stop the clip at 33:44, as Dorothy waves goodbye to the Munchkins.

GROUP

◎ What is your best guess right now of what your "yellow brick road" looks like? Who's traveling it with you?

◎ What "ruby slippers" will you need to keep on your feet as you journey forward? Be specific.

To dig deeper into understanding God's vision for us, here are some great resources:

Holy Discontent: Fueling the Fire That Ignites Personal Vision by Bill Hybels (Zondervan)

Life After Church: God's Call to Disillusioned Christians by Brian Sanders (InterVarsity)

The Irresistible Revolution: Living as an Ordinary Radical by Shane Claiborne (Zondervan)

Visioneering: God's Blueprint for Developing and Maintaining Vision by Andy Stanley (Multnomah)

Let the Nations Be Glad: The Supremacy of God in Missions by John Piper (Baker)

That *Was* You, God...Right?

"*Unless the LORD builds a house, the work of the builders is wasted*" (PSALM 127:1).

In this session, we'll journey...

from → **to**

telling the difference between a good idea and God-given vision...

giving ourselves a "reality check" before taking our real first steps forward.

Before gathering, make sure you have...

- ○ paper for everyone
- ○ pencils with erasers

Optional activities (choose one or both):

Go

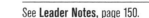

- ○ **Option A:** Discussion (see page 34)
- ○ **Option B:** DVD of *Field of Dreams* (see page 38)

DVD

See **Leader Notes,** page 150.

Come and See

(about 20 minutes)

Have people get in their groups from last week. Give everyone a sheet of paper.

» **Take two minutes to draw a quick floor plan of your dream home—the home you'd build if you could. After two minutes, let someone who didn't lead last week lead this discussion. Compare your floor plans, and then take five minutes to discuss these questions:**

After seven minutes, come back together. Share highlights and insights from the group discussions.

Ask for a volunteer to read Psalm 127:1. Then discuss the questions together:

> *How difficult it is to draw the line with certainty between spiritual wisdom and worldly astuteness!*
>
> —*Dietrich* Bonhoeffer, The Cost of Discipleship

» **Sometimes it's really tough to know how God wants us to step out in faith. Sometimes we want something so badly that we can talk ourselves into believing it's what God wants, too. And maybe it *is* what God wants. But maybe it isn't. And maybe our desire isn't in synch with God's timing, even if it *is* what God wants.**

This session is all about thinking that through—about knowing whether this vision we have is really God's, as well. It's tricky stuff. So let's do our best to check our own desires at the door and discover together what *God* wants.

◎ In what ways are your floor plans similar? How are they different?

◎ How "lost" did you get in imagining your dream home?

◎ How caught up *can* we get in our own dreams? Give examples.

Psalm 127:1

◎ When have you done something believing it was what God wanted and later realized it wasn't? What happened?

◎ Looking back now, what really motivated you?

Seek and Find

(about 20 minutes)

» **Last week, we looked at a case study from the Bible to understand how others before us walked out the vision God gave them. Since this is Session 2, let's go ahead and look at *two* examples this week. Can I have volunteers to read Judges 6:34-40 and 1 Samuel 3:1-19?**

After your volunteers have read, discuss these questions:

"We naively think that the more we grow as Christians, the easier it will be to discern the will of God. But the opposite is often the case. God treats the mature leader as a mature adult, leaving more and more to...spiritual discernment...The resulting perplexity adds inevitably to a leader's pressure."

—J. Oswald Sanders, Spiritual Leadership

"Faith is seeing the invisible, but not the nonexistent."

—A. W. Tozer

 **Judges 6:34-40; 1 Samuel 3:1-19**

◎ How did Gideon and Samuel (and Eli, for that matter) figure out whether it was really God who was speaking?

◎ Would you say any of them showed a lack of faith—or were making wrong demands of God? Why or why not?

◎ Think again about times you mistakenly thought God wanted you to do something. What makes the approaches taken in these passages different from what you did?

◎ Look once more at Gideon's example. When is it OK to "put out a fleece," and when are we just trying to "fleece" ourselves into doing something that's not really God's idea (or get out of doing something that is)?

Go

(about 20 minutes)

> *The first time you receive guidance you will know the difference. You can mistake rhinestones for diamonds, but you can never mistake a diamond for a rhinestone.*
>
> *—Adela Rogers St. Johns*

If you chose **Option A**, *read on.*
If you're doing **Option B**, *go to page 38.*

» **Get back into your groups. Decide who'll lead your discussion. Make sure it's someone who hasn't already led today.** (Pause.)

In our next session, we'll get into what it costs us to step out in faith—what it's going to take to *do* this thing we believe God wants us to do. But today, our focus is on whether these steps really *are* from God—or, for that matter and entirely likely, whether it's both you *and* God, flesh *and* spirit, mixed together right now.

It's critical that we stop to figure out what's God and what's us, because once things get real, we're almost certainly going to find ourselves disagreeing with God on some things. And guess what? God's right. So when that happens, you'll need to remember which parts of this vision are truly God's, so you're able to keep on trusting him when you don't understand what's going on. (And we'll be exploring *that* later this season, too.)

Take a minute to quietly review the questions at the top of your group page. Make sure you write down your answers—you'll want to remember them when you look back over this season. When all of you have finished writing, take turns sharing about which questions are hitting you the hardest right now. You don't need to discuss every question, just the ones connecting with each of you. If there's something else you're wrestling with, discuss that, too.

Discuss the last question as well. Then come up with one action point—one thing you're going to do in response to what God's showing you or to help you sort out exactly what it *is* God's showing you. Make sure you write that down in your Walk It Out section.

Let's plan to come back together in 15 minutes.

Ask yourself:

◎ As I pursue this vision, am I sensing God revealing more about the things he truly cares about?

◎ Will this vision, once it's realized, reveal more about God to others, or will it just reveal more about *me*?

◎ Which parts of this vision were clearly *not* my idea (even if I'm excited about the idea now)?

◎ Have I tried letting go of this idea, only to find God bringing it up again?

◎ Would I want this to happen even if someone else did it—or even if I did it and someone else got the credit?

"This one clear command would redefine you....On those days when things were dark or difficult, you would at least know that you were doing what you were called to do. That clarity...while a heavy burden, would be a great gift to us."

—Brian Sanders, **Life After Church: God's Call to Disillusioned Christians**

◎ Write your thoughts about the above questions here:

◎ What, if anything, do you need right now to be really certain that this vision you're pursuing is really God's idea? If you're certain, *why* are you certain?

Go continued

Come back together as a group. Ask everyone to stand. If possible, get everyone into a more open section of your meeting area, and try to have at least an arm's length between people.

» **Think once more about what you believe God's calling you to do. You might believe without a doubt that it's from God. Or you might still have doubts about whether this is really God's idea or just yours. And that's OK; sometimes being obedient to God means staying put until you're *sure* it's what God wants.**

But now's the time to be honest with God. With everyone's eyes still closed—no one else watching—if you strongly believe that what you're involved with is really from God, take a step forward. Those of you still weighing it out, stay put.

After everyone has stepped (or not stepped) forward, close in prayer.

prayer➔

» **Lord, we thank you because you still speak to us today and because you *want* us to hear your voice more clearly. Sometimes we feel like we're walking blind when we try to follow you. But we know you see what we can't, and we thank you for that.**

We thank you for those who stepped forward, believing they're obeying you by doing so. Continue to confirm and clarify your call to them, and open their eyes to the next steps they need to take.

We also thank you for those who *didn't* step forward and for their desire to be certain it's you they're

Walk It Out

How does what you learned today apply to where you're at right now? How can you put it into practice? Write below one thing you'll do this week to make today's lesson more real in your own life. Share your choices with your group, and make plans to connect before the next session to check in and encourage one another.

Because I want to know God's voice when I hear it (and when I don't), I'll "Walk It Out" by

____

____

____

____

____

____

following. Help them discover in the weeks to come what your will for them truly is. Give them certainty and confidence in you, no matter where you lead them. Help each of us move forward in you, in the path and at the pace you've chosen for each of us. In Jesus' name, amen.

SEEING IT DIFFERENTLY

Go–Option B

LEADER Instead of doing Go as described, try it this way: Watch a scene from *Field of Dreams.* In this scene, Ray Kinsella's hearing things, but why? Cue the movie to 4:18 (DVD Chapter 2), as Ray's walking through the field. Stop the clip at 7:31, after Ray clicks off the TV. Then discuss these questions:

GROUP

◎ Think again about what you believe God's calling you to do. Honestly, how much do you feel like Ray (or Annie) right now? Explain.

◎ What, if anything, do you need right now to be really certain that this vision you're pursuing is really God's idea? If you're certain, *why* are you certain?

Rejoin your groups. Let someone who hasn't led today lead now. (Pause.)

Come up with one action point—one thing you're going to do in response to what God's showing you or to help you sort out exactly what it *is* God's showing you. Write it in your Walk It Out section, and discuss your answers in your group.

Also, be sure to take some time this coming week to think through and write your answers to the questions at the top of page 35. You'll want to remember those answers when you look back over this season.

Let's plan to come back together in five minutes.

Pick up with the prayer.

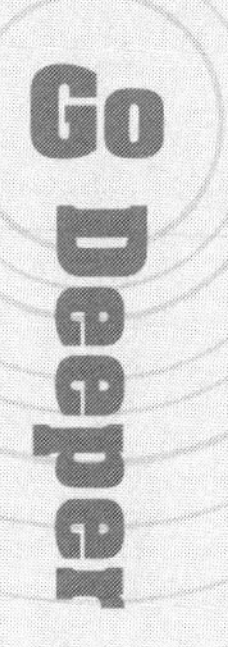

To dig deeper into how to tell God's vision from ours, here are some great resources:

Just Do Something: How to Make a Decision Without Dreams, Visions, Fleeces, Open Doors, Random Bible Verses, Casting Lots, Liver Shivers, Writing in the Sky, etc. by Kevin DeYoung (Moody)

Discovering God's Will: How to Know When You Are Heading in the Right Direction by Andy Stanley (Multnomah)

Holy Hunches: Responding to the Promptings of God by Bruce Main (Baker)

Decision Making and the Will of God: A Biblical Alternative to the Traditional View by Garry Friesen (Multnomah)

Found: God's Will (Find the Direction and Purpose God Wants for Your Life) by John MacArthur, Jr. (Cook)

Counting the ~~Cost~~ Gain

But if I say I'll never mention the LORD or speak in his name, his word burns in my heart like a fire. It's like a fire in my bones! I am worn out trying to hold it in! I can't do it!" (JEREMIAH 20:9).

In this session, we'll journey...

from → **to**

understanding the risks and rewards of pursuing the vision Jesus has given us...

following Jesus' lead, *wherever* he chooses to lead us.

Before gathering, make sure you have...

- ○ a white board or blackboard

Optional activities (choose one or both):

Come and See

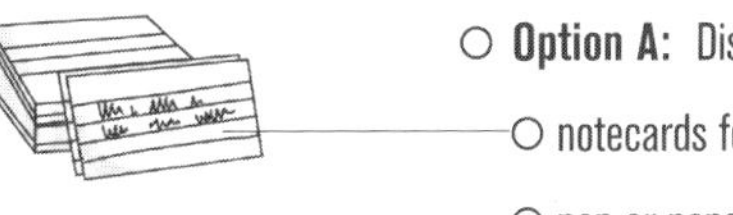

- ○ **Option A:** Discussion (see page 42)
  - ○ notecards for everyone
  - ○ pen or pencil for everyone

- ○ **Option B:** DVD of *The Lord of the Rings: The Fellowship of the Ring* (see page 50)

See **Leader Notes**, page 150.

Come and See

(about 10 minutes)

If you chose **Option A**, *read on.*
If you're doing **Option B**, *go to page 50.*

Have people get into their groups, and give everyone a notecard. Make sure everyone's got something to write with.

» **Here's what you're going to do: Without sharing with anyone else in your group yet, write on the top of your card one irrational fear you have. Then, on the bottom of your card, write a phrase or sentence about a time you feel you showed an unusual amount of courage. When you're done, turn your card over. You'll share this fear with others in a minute.**

Allow about a minute for everyone to write.

» **Now mix your cards up. Let each person draw a card and try to guess who it belongs to. As your identity is revealed, share a little more about your fear and your act of courage.**

Then discuss the questions on your group page together:

After five minutes, bring everyone back together to share highlights and insights from your discussion time.

» **In our last session, we talked about how we can get caught up in wanting something so badly—even if it seems right to *us*—that we can talk ourselves into thinking it's what God wants, too. Let's take that discussion in the opposite direction now:**

> *"Fear of the 'what-ifs' tends to have a strong crippling effect on Christians' outlook and practice. But we're not called to live in fear; we're called to live in faith one day at a time."*
>
> *—Andrew Marin,* Love Is an Orientation

> *"It is a remarkable fact that on this subject Heaven and Hell speak with one voice…What matters, what Heaven desires and Hell fears, is precisely that further step, out of our depth, out of our own control."*
>
> *—C.S. Lewis, "A Slip of the Tongue"*

◎ Which was easier to come up with—a fear or an act of courage? Why?

◎ What drives us to such strong responses, whether it's fear *or* courage?

◎ How can fear and doubt—whether it's about what God wants, our own motives and capabilities, or something else—cause us to miss, or even run away from, what God wants?

Fear of the unknown—or for that matter, of re-experiencing something painful—is something we all face. And because the future *is* unknown, it's easy to make it into something even scarier than it really is.

But while the future is unknown to us, it's not unknown to God. We're here today because we believe there's something God wants *made* known. And for that to happen, the first people who need to see at least part of what God wants made known is us. That thought *should* frighten us. Therefore, we need to get past our own fears of the unknown and trust that God knows where he's taking us.

Last week we ended by taking a symbolic step (or not), to show God whether we felt ready to step forward. This week is about taking a step forward *somehow* and discovering why the step is worth it, despite fears and uncertainty if the step is part of God's vision. So let's begin.

Seek and Find

(about 25 minutes)

The self-tormenting and hopeless question regarding the purity of one's motives, the suspicious observation of oneself, the glaring and fatiguing light of incessant consciousness, all these have nothing to do with the commandment of God, which grants liberty to live and to act.

—*Dietrich Bonhoeffer,* Ethics

» Since this is Session 3, we're going to look at *three* examples this week. (Don't worry, we won't keep upping the ante—no 13 examples by the end of this season.) And since we've already put some of our fears on the table, let's begin to examine the fears we might have about what God's calling us to and how we might get past them. And let's start with an example that few of us would willingly choose. Can someone read Jeremiah 20:7-18?

Write everyone's responses on your white board, but leave room on your white board for later. Then continue your discussion:

Being a disciple to Jesus will again and again get us into situations of trouble that otherwise we could and would have avoided. We must expect it.

—*J.I. Packer and Carolyn Nystrom,* Praying: Finding Our Way Through Duty to Delight

» A big part of recognizing a God-given vision is realizing, "I can't *not* do this." Jeremiah went the distance on a mission that looked like a failure to everyone, including Jeremiah himself. But Jeremiah obeyed God. He even praised God in the midst of his despair, and by doing so, he gave an entire nation an opportunity to turn around.

More often, when God gives a vision, he also provides a happier ending, even though there are huge obstacles to overcome. So let's look at a much more successful—but no less scary—example that took place more than 100 years after Jeremiah's.

Jeremiah 20:7-18

◎ What emotions and reactions does Jeremiah experience here? Name as many as you can.

◎ How can one person possibly be feeling *all* these things at once? How would you explain it?

◎ Where's the "fire in [your] bones" right now? In other words, what would you attempt for God even if you knew you'd fail again and again? And where does the vision you're exploring fit into that?

Seek and Find continued

Over and over, when I ask God why all of these injustices are allowed to exist in the world, I can feel the Spirit whisper to me, 'You tell me why we allow this to happen. You are my body, my hands, my feet.'

—Shane Claiborne, The Irresistible Revolution: Living as an Ordinary Radical

Ask for one or more volunteers to read Nehemiah 1:1–2:8. Then discuss these questions:

Write everyone's responses to this question on your white board, too. Then continue your discussion:

» **There's a certain point where it doesn't matter how hard or impossible something looks—if it's truly God's call, then it's a call we need to answer.**

We never fully know what God's getting us into, and that's often a good thing. Nonetheless, we should make every attempt to understand, to the best of our ability, what God wants and what it's going to cost us. Once we've counted that cost, though, we need to say, "Never mind the cost!" and embrace what God wants to accomplish. God wants to put things right in this world he's created, and he wants us to be a part of that plan.

All the things we value were never meant to be safeguarded. *They were meant to* be put at risk and spent, *for we are in a life-and-death battle.*

—Gary A. Haugen, Just Courage: God's Great Expedition for the Restless Christian

 **Nehemiah 1:1–2:8**

◎ How does Nehemiah seek God's will—and do it—over the course of this passage?

◎ How strong an indication is it that the things we've "wept…mourned, fasted, and prayed to the God of heaven" about are the things God wants us to do? Explain.

◎ What's tougher for you—to weep, mourn, fast, and pray for God's will (see Nehemiah 1:4) or to wait from "late autumn" to "the following spring" (see Nehemiah 1:1 and 2:1) for an answer? Explain.

Go

(about 20 minutes)

Jesus promised the disciples three things—that they would be completely fearless, absurdly happy, and in constant trouble.

—G.K. Chesterton

Two things are apparent: (1) doubt does not negate worship, and (2) worship is the condition of commissioning, not absence of doubt.

—Brian Sanders, Life After Church: God's Call to Disillusioned Christians

» **Let's look at one more example, this time from the New Testament. Can someone read John 6:60-71?**

Get back with your groups now. (Pause.)

You might still be trying to know whether this vision you're wrestling with is God's or not—or whether or not you're meant to be a part of it. So let's wrestle a little more. Discuss the remaining questions on your group page together. The idea here isn't to fast-track, or short-circuit, that wrestling process but to talk and pray about what your next steps are. Because no matter *what* you decide, the future is still unknown, and you'll still need to step *somewhere* with God's help. Write those steps in the Walk It Out section.

When you're done discussing and praying, you're free to leave [or hang out, if you're in a small-group setting]. **May God bless your time together!**

Walk It Out

John 6:60-71

◎ About what in your own life, right now, could you ask, "Jesus, couldn't you have made this a *little* easier to understand?"

◎ How can Peter's response, "Lord, to whom would we go?" help you move forward, even as you continue to work through those things you don't understand?

◎ Which of today's three passages feels closest to your situation right now? Why?

◎ If things don't turn out the way *you* envisioned, what's the benefit of following wherever Jesus takes you anyway?

Because I need to realize how far Jesus wants me to go—and then still *go there*—I'll "Walk It Out" by

___

___

___

SEEING IT DIFFERENTLY

Come and See–Option B

LEADER Instead of the notecard activity in Come and See, watch a scene from the movie *The Lord of the Rings: The Fellowship of the Ring*. Cue the movie to 35:10 (DVD Chapter 8), as Gandalf tells Frodo, "You'll have to leave the name of Baggins behind you."

» **We're going to start this session with a movie clip. As you watch, put yourself in this scene and think about the mission *you're* feeling called to right now.**

Start your clip, and then stop it at 38:20, as the voice of Bilbo Baggins says, "...there's no knowing *where* you might be swept off to."

GROUP

◎ Who in this scene do you feel most like right now? Why?

◎ What do you think of Bilbo's words at the end? Do they comfort you, unsettle you, or do something in between?

Pick up at the leader statement near the bottom of page 42 beginning, **"In our last session, we talked about how we can get caught up in wanting something so badly..."**

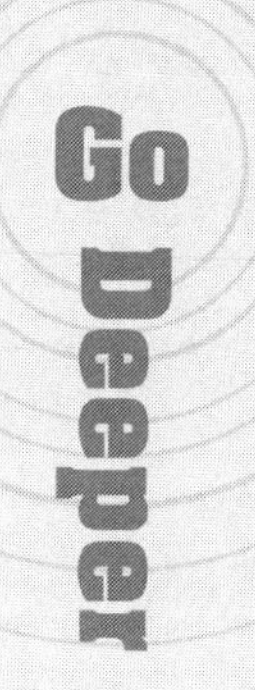

To learn more about stepping into the deep end, here are some great resources:

Hope Lives: A Journey of Restoration by Amber Van Schooneveld (Group)

Crazy Love: Overwhelmed by a Relentless God by Francis Chan (Cook)

The Danger Habit: How to Grow Your Love of Risk into Life-Changing Faith by Mike Barrett (Multnomah)

The Crime of Living Cautiously: Hearing God's Call to Adventure by Luci Shaw (InterVarsity)

Take the Risk: Learning to Identify, Choose, and Live with Acceptable Risk by Ben Carson (Zondervan)

Of *Course* My Family Supports This (Don't They?)

"Jesus asked, 'Who is my mother? Who are my brothers?' Then he pointed to his disciples and he said, 'Look, these are my mother and brothers. Anyone who does the will of my Father in heaven is my brother and sister and mother!' " (MATTHEW 12:48-50).

In this session, we'll journey...

from exploring the importance of sharing God's vision with our families...

to helping both ourselves and our families embrace the changes and cooperation it requires.

Before gathering, make sure you have...

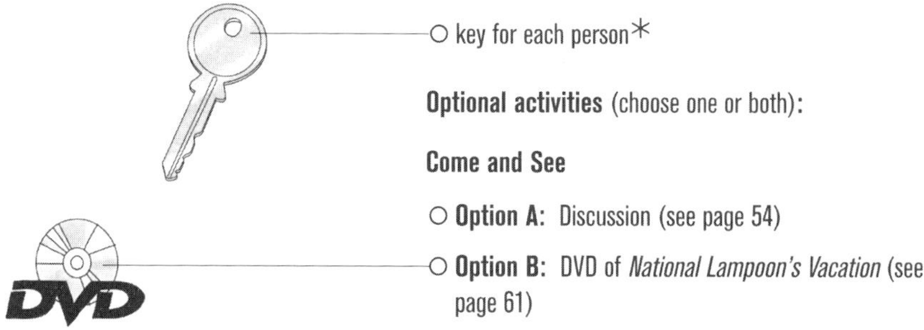

○ key for each person*

Optional activities (choose one or both):

Come and See

○ **Option A:** Discussion (see page 54)

○ **Option B:** DVD of *National Lampoon's Vacation* (see page 61)

*See **Leader Notes**, page 151, for details.

Come and See

(about 10 minutes)

If you chose **Option A**, *read on.*
If you're doing **Option B**, *go to page 61.*

» Get in your groups, and discuss these questions:

Come back together after five minutes to discuss highlights and insights from your discussion time.

» Sometimes we look back at disagreements we've had with our families and laugh. Sometimes the disagreements were so painful that we *still* don't want to think about them. But our families' support for what God's trying to do in our lives can be essential. To put it bluntly, if we can't communicate to those closest to us that we believe the vision is from God, and how much we need *their* support, how can we honestly expect *anyone else's* support?

Depending on our situations, we might *not* be able to expect our families to support or even understand what God's calling us to. But our spouses, our children, and our extended families can still serve as a reality check. They may not see what God's doing in our lives, but they see *us*. And no matter how painful or seemingly unfair their concerns might be, they might well have a grain of truth. Now's the time to deal with those grains.

Sometimes we just need to help those we care about see what we're seeing. The unknown *is* scary. We wouldn't have spent the past three sessions addressing that if it weren't true. So let's discover how we can help our families see and embrace what God puts on our hearts.

◎ When have you told your family about something you really wanted to do—but *they* didn't (and/or didn't want you to do it either)? How did it work out?

◎ What might have helped them—or you—make the right decision?

Seek and Find

(about 30 minutes)

» **But first, let's look at a biblical example of one family venture gone terribly wrong. Can someone read Genesis 19:1-4, 9-38?**

Think about your family and the "God things" we've been trying to sort out together for the past month. Now think about sharing your own God thing with people in your family—or think about what you've shared with them already—and let's talk this through a little further:

Let's look now at a very different example—one that, in fact, involved Lot's extended family. Can someone else read Genesis 22:1-18?

 **Genesis 19:1-4, 9-38**

◎ What's motivating each family member here, and what went wrong for each of them?

◎ Why didn't Lot's family just listen to him—let alone to God's angels?

◎ What parts of your personality or behavior might cause family members to respond "Yeah, *right*" to what you're sharing? Do they have a point? If so, why?

Genesis 22:1-18

◎ What do you think is going through Abraham's and Isaac's heads here?

◎ Most of us don't have family members as compliant as Isaac, even when they love and want to support us. How can we help them deal with the fears and hesitancy they still might have?

◎ Which of the two situations we've looked at seems most like yours? Explain.

◎ What *do* you think you and your family will need to sacrifice as you follow God's vision? How easy or difficult will it be for all of you to believe that God will provide what's needed for *your* sacrifice?

Go

(about 20 minutes)

> *The darkest place of any lighthouse is always at its base. The same can be said of too many ministry families. Let it not be so! Fight for your family. If you miss that home base, you will have nowhere to go when your ministry days are over.*
>
> *—Wayne Cordeiro*

» **We've probably all heard the phrase, "If Momma ain't happy, ain't nobody happy." But what we're considering isn't just about Momma (or wives). The family members whose support we need could be our husbands, children, parents, or anyone else we're close to. This is an issue that *literally* hits close to home. In a sense, you're asking your family to show even more faith than you have—because they're needing to trust not only God but also *you*.**

And this can get complicated in a hurry. We want to please God. And we want our families to be happy. Even the Bible can give us what seem to be conflicting messages about this. Let's look at some of those messages and try to make some sense of them.

Get into your groups. Read the passages listed on your group page, and then discuss the questions that follow. When you're done, move on to Walk It Out and share what you'll do in response to today's session. Let's plan to come back together in 15 minutes.

- Matthew 12:46-50
- Luke 14:25-33
- 1 Corinthians 7:29-35
- Ephesians 5:28–6:4

Walk It Out

Get back into your groups. Let someone who hasn't led yet lead this piece.

How does what you've learned today apply to where you are right now? How can you put it into practice? Take five minutes in your groups to write one thing you'll do this week to make today's lesson more real in your own life. Share your choices with your group, and make plans to connect before the next session to check in and encourage one another other.

Matthew 12:46-50; Luke 14:25-33; 1 Corinthians 7:29-35; Ephesians 5:28–6:4

◎ How do we reconcile these passages? How can we follow Jesus *and* honor our families?

◎ What does that look like to you right now? What specific actions will you need to take to make it happen?

Because God's vision affects my family, too, I'll "Walk It Out" by

____

____

____

____

Go continued

Come back together as a group.

» **I'd like all of you to take out your keys. Hold up the key that you consider your most important one.**

Give a key to anyone who doesn't have one.

» **Keys do a lot of things. They open things; they lock things away and protect them; they turn things on and off. I'd like you to think about the key you're holding and about today's session. What's God asking you to do in relation to your family? Do you need to open up and share more of what's really on your heart? Protect what God's showing you from the criticism of an unbelieving family? Or just get in the car and take a long drive with your spouse or child who's afraid of losing your time and attention?**

Whatever comes to mind, hold up your key and pray silently about it for a minute. I'll close in prayer and give you a chance to add your prayers out loud. Let's meditate and pray about what God's showing each of us right now.

After a minute, begin praying out loud for your group.

prayer ➔

» **Lord, we want to be obedient to you in every part of our lives. We want our families to understand and support what you're showing us and to help us see our own blind spots. We lift up our needs to you right now, Lord.**

Allow time for everyone to share. Add your own request out loud. Give others the chance to join in. Once everyone's had a chance to share, close your prayer time.

» **Help us do everything in our power to love our families and reveal your will to them as we continue to seek your will no matter what the reactions might be. Give us patience to wait for our families, if that's what's needed. Give them patience with us. Help us all follow you no matter what fears or misunderstandings there might be in the meantime. In Jesus' name, amen.**

SEEING IT DIFFERENTLY

LEADER Instead of the small-group discussion in Come and See, watch a scene together from the movie *National Lampoon's Vacation*. Cue the movie to 5:15 (DVD Chapter 3), as the station wagon pulls into the driveway. Stop the clip at 8:24, after Clark says, "Why aren't we flying? Because getting there is half the fun. *You* know *that*."

Stay together as a larger group, and pick up at the questions in Come and See on page 55.

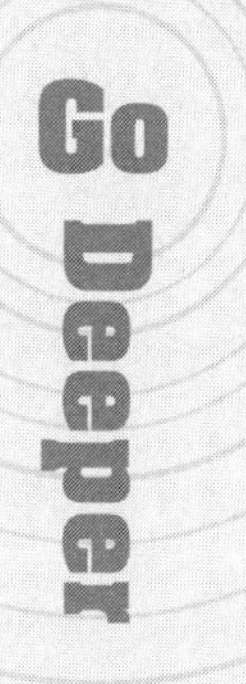

To dig deeper into how to invest in your family as you invest further in God's kingdom, here are some great resources:

The Dream Releasers: How to Help Others Realize Their Dreams While Achieving Your Own by Wayne Cordeiro (Regal)

Choosing to Cheat: Who Wins When Family and Work Collide? by Andy Stanley (Multnomah)

Sacred Marriage by Gary Thomas (Zondervan)

The Pilgrim's Progress by John Bunyan (various publishers)

Can I Pray for You?

"*Don't worry about anything; instead, pray about everything. Tell God what you need, and thank him for all he has done. Then you will experience God's peace, which exceeds anything we can understand. His peace will guard your hearts and minds as you live in Christ Jesus*" (PHILIPPIANS 4:6-7).

In this session, we'll journey...

from → **to**

understanding that we always need to seek God's help and guidance in prayer...

finding others who'll help us seek God's will and guidance.

Before gathering, make sure you have...

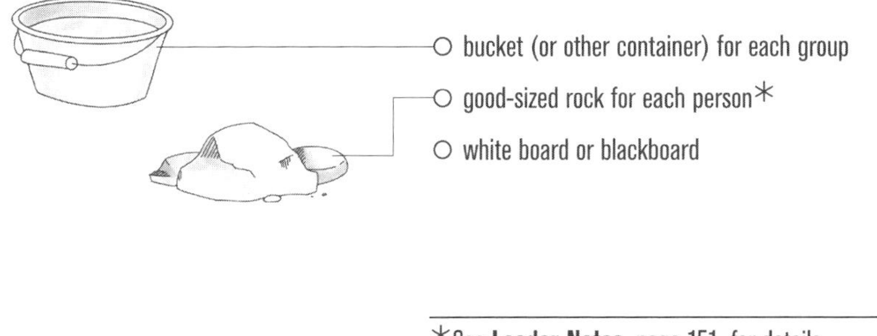

- ○ bucket (or other container) for each group
- ○ good-sized rock for each person*
- ○ white board or blackboard

*See **Leader Notes**, page 151, for details.

Come and See

(about 10 minutes)

Be sure to open your session in prayer, if you don't already.

» While prayer is something we all do—or maybe *because* it is—it can become something we take for granted. We can go through the motions and forget the awesome power prayer has. So today, let's look at this subject through fresh eyes and discover how our prayers can play a much bigger role as we dive deeper into the plans God has for us.

Take a minute to read the two quotes on your group page to yourselves, and then we'll talk.

We're at a point now, or will be soon, where we need to share what God has been putting on our hearts. And because it's a God thing, prayer isn't just a nice add-on. It's our lifeline. It's our ultimate reality check with the Ultimate Reality. It's also our way of connecting others with God's work in a way that helps them see that it *is* God's work. So let's explore how we can engage with God more deeply in prayer and how we can invite others along on this journey.

> *Tomorrow I plan to work, work, from early until late. In fact I have so much to do that I shall spend the first three hours in prayer.*
>
> *—Martin Luther*

> *Do you and I have work that we can't imagine doing for thirty minutes without prayer? If not, perhaps we need a new life's work. Or perhaps we need to do an old life's work in a new way.*
>
> *—Gary Haugen,*
> **Just Courage: God's Great Expedition for the Restless Christian**

◎ What are your reactions to these quotes? Explain.

◎ How have *your* prayers changed over the past month as God has been affirming and expanding the vision he's given you?

Seek and Find

(about 30 minutes)

> *If we do not yearn and pray and expect God to stretch out his hand and do the supernatural, it will not happen. That is the simple truth of the matter. We must give him room to operate.*
>
> —Jim Cymbala, Fresh Wind, Fresh Fire

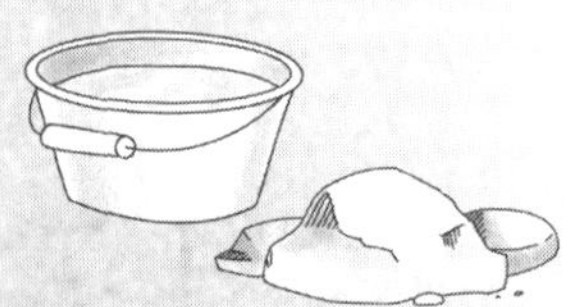

Ask for a volunteer to read Matthew 7:7-11.

» **God has given us a mission in this world. But although God gave it to us, it's still *God's* mission. God is our ultimate authority. God will give us what we ask for—or very likely, something even better, even if we don't recognize the fact that it's even better right away. God's power and God's provision go together.**

Let's investigate one example. Can someone read Acts 4, verses 13 and 18-35?

Most of us would welcome support of any kind, whether it's prayer or encouragement or the meeting of a tangible need. But often, getting support requires letting go of some pride and *allowing* ourselves to be supported. It means being open about what our real needs are. But the benefits far outweigh a temporarily bruised pride or our fear of admitting we need help.

You've probably already noticed the buckets and rocks. Now we're going to put you to work.

Get into your groups. Decide who's the strongest person in your group (no fighting over it!). That person will load up your bucket with a rock for each one of you and bring it to where you're gathering. The same person will also lead your discussion time.

Allow time for people to get into their groups and for the rock carriers to load up their buckets.

» **Read Philippians 4:6-7. Then each take a rock and hold on to it as you discuss these questions together. Leave your empty bucket in the middle of your group.**

Let's take 10 minutes to discuss.

Regain everyone's attention after 10 minutes, keeping people with their groups. Share highlights and insights from the discussion time.

Acts 4:13, 18-35

◎ How do you see others catch and spread the vision by "[being] with Jesus" either in prayer or, in Peter and John's case, physically?

◎ What connections do you see between our prayers and our willingness to help others?

◎ What needs do you see around you right now that need to be prayed about—and met?

Philippians 4:6-7

◎ Where are you struggling to find God's peace right now? What's the need behind that struggle?

◎ Why do we hold onto our needs—the way we're holding on to our rocks—instead of immediately giving them to God? Why do we often forget to thank God *after* we've given those needs to him?

◎ How could we catch ourselves earlier, so we can share our needs—and our gratitude—sooner?

Go

(about 20 minutes)

Reminder: People should still be sitting with their groups, although they'll participate in the following discussion as a larger group.

Ask for volunteers to read Matthew 18:19-20 and Colossians 4:12-13, and then discuss these questions:

Write everyone's answers to this question on your white board. Then continue your discussion:

» We need people in our lives who are as faithfully seeking God's will for us as we are. We need people we can be vulnerable with, so they know how to pray for us—and help us. And as our relationships deepen, we'll be able to help each other in ways that only God could have made possible because we'll have invited God into every step of it. And the people you're with right now may be just the people to start with.

prayer **So, let's start practicing. Open up a little (or more) to each other about what, if anything, is really weighing you down right now. As you share your prayer request, hold up your rock as a physical reminder of the weight of your burden. Once you're done with your prayer request, put your rock—your burden—back in the bucket. Then take turns lifting those burdens up to God. Leave some silences between your prayers, so you can listen for God's answers together.**

Let someone who hasn't already led today lead this time together. When you're done praying, you're free to leave [or hang out, if you're in a small group].

Walk It Out

How does what you learned today apply to where you are right now? How can you put it into practice? Write one thing you'll do this week to make today's lesson more real in your own life. Share your choices with your group, and make plans to connect before the next session to check in and encourage one another.

Matthew 18:19-20; Colossians 4:12-13

◎ What are the benefits of others praying with us and for us? Come up with as many ideas as you can, either from these passages or your own experiences.

◎ Who's *your* Epaphras, and why?

◎ How could having a group of Christ followers like Epaphras in your life help you grow in your mission?

Because there's power in numbers seeking God's will for me, I'll "Walk It Out" by

____

____

____

To dig deeper into how to speak to God about his vision—and finding others who'll help—here are some great resources:

Operation World by Patrick Johnstone and Jason Mandryk (Gabriel)

Power Through Prayer by E.M. Bounds (CreateSpace)

The Ministry of Intercessory Prayer by Andrew Murray (Bethany House)

Let the Nations Be Glad: The Supremacy of God in Missions by John Piper (Baker)

Sharing the Vision

"Then Jesus gave them this illustration: 'No one tears a piece of cloth from a new garment and uses it to patch an old garment. For then the new garment would be ruined, and the new patch wouldn't even match the old garment.

"'And no one puts new wine into old wineskins. For the new wine would burst the wineskins, spilling the wine and ruining the skins. New wine must be stored in new wineskins. But no one who drinks the old wine seems to want the new wine. "The old is just fine," they say'" (LUKE 5:36-39).

In this session, we'll journey...

from → **to**

addressing the obstacles that block sharing the vision God has shared with us...

understanding how we can best communicate that vision to others.

Before gathering, make sure you have...

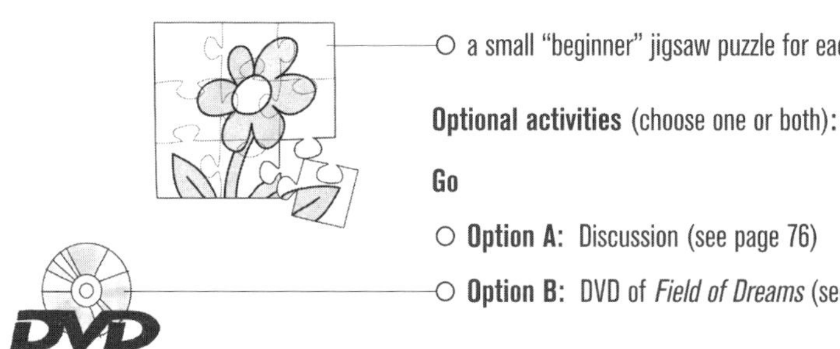

○ a small "beginner" jigsaw puzzle for each group*

Optional activities (choose one or both):

Go

○ **Option A:** Discussion (see page 76)

○ **Option B:** DVD of *Field of Dreams* (see page 79)

*See **Leader Notes**, page 151, for details.

Come and See

(about 15 minutes)

Have people get into their groups, and give each group a puzzle.

» Take a few minutes to assemble your puzzle. As you put the pieces together, take turns sharing about a time you couldn't "see the big picture"—a painful time that something positive came out of or a promise you had to wait for, for example.

Once you've completed your puzzle, take a few moments to admire your work, and then take 10 minutes to discuss these questions:

After 10 minutes, bring everyone back together. Share highlights and insights from your discussion time.

» In our last session, we discussed the importance of finding others we can be open with—others who can support us in prayer and by doing whatever God puts on their hearts to do as a result of those prayers.

Now we take this one step further. It's time to bring this vision out in the open where even more people can see it—and hopefully become a part of it in some way. This is a big and often tricky step. By putting ourselves out there, we're opening ourselves up to people we pretty much can guarantee won't catch the vision right away. But as we share what's really moving us—*Who's* really moving us—we also develop new relationships. People get the opportunity to see where they fit into this new thing. Real needs get revealed. And as relationships develop, others begin to get excited about what God wants to do—maybe even to the point of letting go of whatever fears or established ways of doing things might be holding *them* back.

So let's begin by sharing today and see where we go from there.

> *"If it is that difficult to describe something perceived through the senses, imagine how much harder it is to put words around what does not come through the senses! The language of God is like this."*
>
> *—St. John of the Cross,* Dark Night of the Soul

◎ Think about the stories you just shared. How did you handle waiting while those events were taking place? What was it like trying to explain to others what you were going through?

◎ What was it like when the pieces finally fell into place? What or who helped you while you waited for that to happen?

Seek and Find

(about 20 minutes)

> *One of the greatest pains to human nature is the pain of a new idea. It... makes you think that after all, your favorite notions may be wrong, your firmest beliefs ill-founded... Naturally, therefore, common men hate a new idea, and are disposed more or less to ill-treat the original man who brings it.*
>
> —*Walter Bagehot,* Physics and Politics

» It's not easy for others to understand what God's showing us. It probably hasn't been easy for *us* to get what God's showing us, and we've probably been at it a lot longer. So let's look at an example of someone else about to "go public" with what God showed him and then explore what that struggle might look like for us.

Ask for volunteers to read Exodus 3:7-14; 4:1-14; and 4:28-31, and then discuss the questions:

» It's important that you share not just the plans in our heads, but also the burden God has put on your heart. Plans will change. The people around you will change. Even the focus of what you *think* this vision was about may shift. But whatever truly comes from God will survive *all* those changes. Make *that* the center as you share, and don't ever *leave* that center. Let God sort out the details. And let's move on.

> *In the absence of a vision, there are nightmares.*
>
> —*Bruce Cockburn, "Night Train"*

 **Exodus 3:7-14; 4:1-14, 28-31**

◎ Truthfully, how much does this feel like where you're at right now? Why?

◎ How did God reassure Moses that his message *will* be heard?

◎ How might our anticipation of people's reactions affect what and how we share? Come up with both positive and negative examples.

◎ What parts of your vision are you sure are God's, too? How can keeping the focus there, rather than on your own ideas, help you share more effectively?

Go

(about 20 minutes)

If you chose **Option A**, *read on.*
If you're doing **Option B**, *go to page 79.*

» **Let's look at a passage that will help us better see this issue from the other side—the side we're trying to reach. As our volunteer reads, think about how this might affect the way you share God's vision. Can someone read Luke 5:36-39?**

Get back into your groups. (Pause.)

We've talked a lot about vision in this session. So let's wrap up by putting some of our talk into practice. Take turns presenting your vision to each other in no-more-than-one-minute statements. Be as clear and simple as possible.

After each person shares, take another minute as a group to give that person feedback. What helped each of you understand the vision? What got in the way of understanding? What didn't that person say that *needed* to be said?

Once everyone's had a chance to share, move on to Walk It Out and share with one another what steps you'll take this week to begin making God's vision real to others. Let's come back together in 15 minutes.

Walk It Out

How does what you've learned today apply to where you're at right now? How can you put it into practice? Take five minutes in your groups to write one thing you'll do this week to make today's lesson more real in your own life. Share your choices with your group, and make plans to connect before the next session to check in and encourage one another.

Luke 5:36-39

◎ What specific resistance do you expect from others as you share this new thing? What's "just fine" about the old things that might get defended as you share?

◎ How can you validate what others have already done while showing them the need for change?

◎ How willing are *you* to change so that you can walk others through this vision in a way that helps them see it? What will that look like?

Because I'm the flesh who needs to be put on God's vision so others can see it, I'll "Walk It Out" by

____

____

____

Go continued

prayer Come back together as a group. Lead your group in prayer, asking God to show each person how he or she can make God's vision real to the people who need to hear it. Ask God to break down resistance, that both sides would be able to open their hearts further to this new thing God wants to do in their midst.

To dig deeper into how to effectively communicate God's vision, here are some great resources:

An Unstoppable Force: Daring to Become the Church God Had in Mind by Erwin Raphael MacManus (Group)

The Power of Vision: Discover and Apply God's Vision for Your Life and Ministry by George Barna (Regal)

Communicating for a Change: Seven Keys to Irresistible Communication by Andy Stanley and Lane Jones (Multnomah)

Developing a Vision for Ministry in the 21st Century by Aubrey Malphurs (Baker)

SEEING IT DIFFERENTLY

Go–Option B

LEADER Instead of the reading and discussion of Luke 5 in Go, watch a scene from *Field of Dreams.* Cue the movie to 1:20:49 (DVD Chapter 28), as Mark pulls up to the ball field. Stop the clip at 1:29:27, as Mark staggers back to the house, muttering "Don't sell the farm, Ray." (Note: Mark uses the word *hell* at 1:23:10, and *damn* at 1:26:29; keep the mute button handy if you need to use it.)

GROUP

- What "realities" did Ray have to look past to keep sight of his vision?
- What did it take for the vision to become real to Mark?
- What risks or sacrifices might you need to make to show how much you believe in God's vision, so others can believe it, too?

Pick up at the prompt, **"Get back into your groups,"** on page 76.

Follow *Me?*

"*As Jesus was walking along, he saw a man named Matthew sitting at his tax collector's booth. 'Follow me and be my disciple,' Jesus said to him. So Matthew got up and followed him"* (MATTHEW 9:9).

In this session, we'll journey...

from → **to**

exploring the challenges of sharing a vision on a more personal level...

identifying the people we'll invite to help shape this vision and discovering how to invite them.

Before gathering, make sure you have...

Optional activities (choose one or both):

Seek and Find

○ **Option A:** Opening discussion (see page 84)

DVD

○ **Option B:** DVD of *Dances With Wolves* (see page 88)

See **Leader Notes**, page 152.

Come and See

(about 10 minutes)

I used to teach that vision is a clear, compelling magnetic image of a preferable future…Then I got involved in actual leading. Since then I've discovered that vision is more like a compass than a roadmap. It provides direction; it guides; it motivates toward a desirable future.

—Rick Rusaw and Eric Swanson, The Externally Focused Church

» **We wrapped up our last session by looking at Jesus' words about new wineskins and the challenges we'll need to face when the old meets the new. Let's begin this session by picking up that thought and carrying it a little further. But first, please get into your groups.**

Give groups time to assemble.

» **Think about a time *you* began something that was brand-new, although you thought you already understood it. For instance, maybe you moved to a new town, began a new job, or began attending a new church. Then take five minutes to discuss these questions together:**

After five minutes, bring everyone back together to share highlights and insights from the discussions.

» **Today we're going to think through how to invite and transition others into the work God has called us to. For many of you, this is even more important than your ability to share with a bigger group, because this is where you'll identify the people who'll walk most closely with you as you follow God's vision together. This is also the stage where you'll be able to identify what the real issues are—the fears, the gaps in your plans, the old things people need to let go of to embrace this new thing. It's an opportunity to invite others to help you think things through, even if they don't join you. Let's begin by looking at people who helped start something new a long time ago.**

◎ What skills and experiences were you able to use in your new situation? What "great ideas" from your past just didn't work?

◎ What did you learn from that time of transition?

Seek and Find

(about 20 minutes)

If you chose **Option A**, *read on.*
If you're doing **Option B**, *go to page 88.*

» **But first, let's lighten the discussion a bit. If you're here, you probably know a decent amount about the disciples by now. So let's discuss these questions:**

Let's look at how Jesus invited the disciples to join *him*. Can I have volunteers to read Matthew 4:18-22; Matthew 9:9; and John 1:35-50?

◎ Which disciple is your favorite and why?

◎ Which disciple do you think would have been the hardest for you to deal with? Why? (And no, you can't say "Judas.")

◎ What did everyone's response tell you about the kinds of people Jesus is willing to use—even within this room?

Matthew 4:18-22; 9:9; John 1:43-50

◎ What common threads do you find in Jesus' invitations? How do you see Jesus tweaking his invitation, depending on who he was giving it to?

◎ There are a *lot* of things Jesus doesn't say here. Why do you think he doesn't say them?

◎ Is inviting others to join in God's work really as simple as Jesus makes it look? Are we the ones who make it complicated? Explain your answers.

Go

(about 30 minutes)

» **OK, so we're not recruiting disciples, at least not in the sense Jesus was. But as we've been discussing these questions—and probably long before—you've likely been thinking of people you want to say "Follow me" to. So let's begin to really process this.**

First, on your own, take 10 minutes to write the names of the people you want to talk to. Then think about and write your answers to the questions that follow your list.

Allow 10 minutes for everyone to write.

» **Now, take 15 minutes to discuss your answers with one another in your groups. Help each other really dig into this. Make time outside this session, if you need more time to talk it out.**

When you're done discussing, take a few more minutes to pray for the specific people, needs, and challenges you've each brought up today. After you've finished praying, you're free to leave [or quietly hang out, if it's a small-group environment].

Walk It Out

How does what you learned today apply to where you are right now? How can you put it into practice? Write one thing you'll do this week to make today's lesson more real in your own life. Share your choices with your group, and make plans to connect before the next session to check in and encourage each other.

These are the people I want to ask to follow me:

◎ What gets each of these people excited about Jesus?

◎ How will I need to change my approach for each person—or do I just *say* it?

◎ How can I invite them into helping me think this vision through, whether or not they join the team?

Because it's people who make a vision come to life, I'll "Walk It Out" by

____

____

____

____

SEEING IT DIFFERENTLY

Seek and Find–Option B

LEADER Instead of the opening discussion in Seek and Find, watch a scene from *Dances With Wolves*. Cue the movie to 1:03:06 (Chapter 9), as Stands With a Fist is digging. Stop the clip at 1:05:43, as Black Shawl goes into the teepee.

GROUP

- Where did Kicking Bird go wrong in his attempt to recruit Stands With a Fist? What would you have done differently?

- Think about the mission you're involved in and the specific people you want to talk to about it. How might "the difficulty [be] yours"? What in your communication style might keep others from hearing your message clearly or be willing to listen to it?

Pick up on page 84 with, **"Let's look at how Jesus invited the disciples to join *him*."**

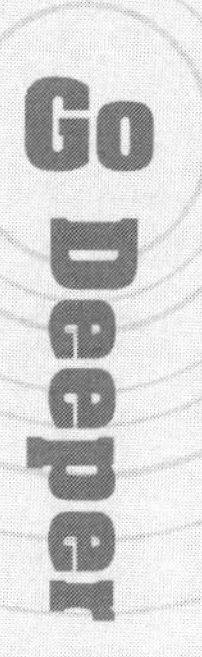

To dig deeper into how to invite others to join in following God's vision with you, here are some great resources:

The New Breed: Understanding and Equipping the 21st Century Volunteer by Jonathan R. McKee and Thomas W. McKee (Group)

The Volunteer Revolution: Unleashing the Power of Everybody by Bill Hybels (Zondervan)

Simply Strategic Volunteers: Empowering People for Ministry by Tony Morgan and Tim Stevens (Group)

Whole Church: Leading from Fragmentation to Engagement by Mel Lawrenz (Jossey-Bass)

Grow, Team!

"*Is there any encouragement from belonging to Christ? Any comfort from his love? Any fellowship together in the Spirit? Are your hearts tender and compassionate? Then make me truly happy by agreeing wholeheartedly with each other, loving one another, and working together with one mind and purpose*" (PHILIPPIANS 2:1-2).

In this session, we'll journey...

from → **to**

from	to
knowing that a good team makes a vision happen...	discovering how to enjoy and expand the teams God has put us on.

Before gathering, make sure you have...

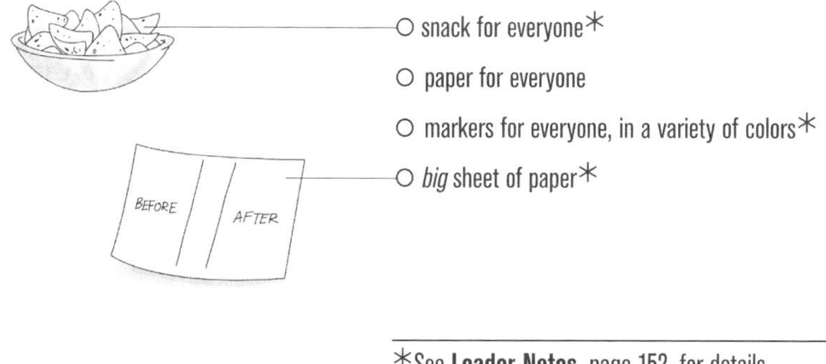

- ○ snack for everyone*
- ○ paper for everyone
- ○ markers for everyone, in a variety of colors*
- ○ *big* sheet of paper*

*See **Leader Notes**, page 152, for details.

Come and See

(about 10 minutes)

» **We've covered a lot these first several weeks, so let's relax and enjoy each other's company a little before digging deeper today. Help yourself to a snack. Then instead of getting with your group, find another person who's not in your group to sit with and discuss these questions with as you eat:**

Everyone knows how difficult it is for Christians to live together! When by the grace of God it happens, and continues to happen, even hell takes notice.

—*Watchman Nee,* Changed into His Likeness

Bring everyone back together after five minutes to share highlights or insights from the discussions.

» **If you haven't already guessed, we're going to look at the importance of teamwork, and we're going to have some fun today doing that. The people you pursue a God-given vision with are the people who will make this vision real to everyone else, and the more life you share with them, the more life your vision will take on.**

Your team isn't just a group of people trying to accomplish a task; you're friends working toward a common vision. And friends have fun together, too. Sometimes fun is *exactly* what you need to become closer and move forward together. So let's have some fun today, and see how far we've already come together.

◎ What's your favorite team or organization? Why?

◎ What's the best team, organization, or group you've been a part of? What made it such a positive experience?

Seek and Find

(about 25 minutes)

Give everyone a piece of paper; make sure everyone has something to write with.

» **For the next three minutes, you'll be discovering what you have in common with others in this room. And you're going to have to talk to each other to find out what those things are. Maybe you like the same kind of music, the same foods, or the same activities. So find a partner and *ask.***

You can't take the cheap way out and talk about physical features. "We both have blue eyes" or "We both have noses" won't work. Discover something new about the actual *person* you're talking with.

Once you and your partner have come up with something you have in common, find someone else to pair up with and discover something you have in common with the new partner. Then go on to the next person. You can't use the same thing twice; it has to be something unique to the pair you're in.

You have three minutes to come up with as many matches as you can. Go!

Give a warning when 30 seconds are remaining. When time is up, find out who has the longest list and give him or her a round of applause. Then discuss: ______

» **Let's look at other ways we can build teamwork as Christians. Today we're not going to break down a Bible story for our case study, but we *are* going to look at a longer passage Paul wrote to encourage a specific church. From there, we'll work through what Paul's advice might mean to us. Can someone read Romans 12:3-13?** ______

Write responses you receive to the last two questions in the middle column of the large sheet of paper (see Leader Notes).

> *"Christian brotherhood is not an ideal which we must realize; it is rather a reality created by God in Christ in which we may participate."*
>
> *—Dietrich Bonhoeffer,* Life Together

◎ How easy or difficult was it to discover things you have in common?

◎ What activity might you be able to do with someone you talked with, based on what you discovered together?

 **Romans 12:3-13**

◎ Which of the roles Paul talks about in verses 6-8 best describes you? Which of your current (or potential) teammates show evidence of other gifts mentioned?

◎ Look again at verses 9-13. Who do you know who excels in some of the specific character qualities listed here? Talk a little about him or her.

◎ Think about the teammates pursuing this vision with you. What else do you already have in common? How could you use what you have in common to build up your team?

◎ How could you celebrate the variety of gifts, passions, and qualities in your team members? Be specific.

Go

(about 25 minutes)

> *It has been said that true friendship begins only when people share a common memory and can say to each other, 'Do you remember?' Each of us [Christian disciples] is one of a great fellowship of people who share a common experience and a common memory of their Lord.*
>
> —*William Barclay,* The Daily Study Bible

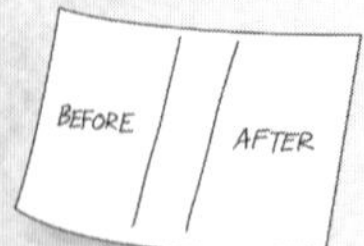

» **Before our next activity, let's take a quick step back, exhale, and think about a few things we may have forgotten or overlooked during the course of this season.**

First, think about this study you're holding, the one we're working through together. Then consider the fact that people around the country are either working through this right now or have worked through it. So you're already part of a much bigger group. And you're part of a *far* bigger group than that. You're part of Jesus' church. The church *he* started. The church he's been renewing the vision of for centuries. The church he's coming back for.

The vision you're a part of is going to get bigger, too. As that happens, you'll draw more and more people onto your team, and that will mean sharing the vision and allowing it to expand with each person you share it with.

So we're going to have a little more fun today making that idea come to life. We've talked a lot about sharing the big picture. But today—with this entire group as our team—we're going to *make* a big picture. And all of you are going to contribute.

Each of you will draw two pictures. Don't worry about your artistic ability or the lack thereof. On the "Before" side, draw a picture that illustrates your church or ministry today. Your second picture, on the "After" side, should represent what you believe your church could be in the future as a result of the vision God has planted in you. Make sure there's a connection between your Before and After pictures.

◎ What do your Before and After frames tell you about how we currently view the church—and about the kind of church we envision?

◎ What did you discover about each other through the pictures and visions we shared?

◎ What connections do you see among the different pictures people drew? What does that suggest about what God can do with the teams you're on?

You'll have 10 minutes to make your contributions to our poster. So grab a marker, and get started.

After 10 minutes, bring everyone back together. Ask for a few volunteers to share about their drawings.

» **You've all brought a lot of vision to the table—or, more specifically, to our wall. So let's take a good look at our entire Before picture.** (Pause.)

Now, let's give our After picture a good once-over. (Pause.) **Now, let's discuss.**

Go continued

Ask for a volunteer to read Philippians 2:1-3.

» **Take another look at the column in the middle of our big picture, and let's discuss this: ___**

After a minute of silence, close your group time in prayer.

» **You've been away from your regular teams long enough. Get into your groups now, and do your Walk It Out time together. We'll come back for prayer afterward.**

Come back together as a group.

prayer

» **We've had a lot of fun today. But we don't want to just have a good time and walk away. We're all part of a team here, so let's reflect once more on that. I'll read Philippians 2:1-3 again. Close your eyes and listen quietly, and then I'll close us in prayer.**

Read Philippians 2:1-3, and then close your group's prayer time. Ask God to give each person a deeper sense of belonging to one another—and a deeper sense of how much everyone belongs to Jesus. Ask God to open each person's eyes to new opportunities to connect and to help each other allow God to take those connections as far as he wants to.

Walk It Out

Get back into your groups. Let someone who hasn't led yet lead this piece.

How does what you learned today apply to where you're at right now? How can you put it into practice? Take five minutes in your groups to write one thi you'll do this week to make today's lesson more real in your own life. Share yo choices with your group, and make plans to connect before the next session to check in and encourage one another.

 **Philippians 2:1-3**

◎ Which of these ideas do you think would work best right now to get your team "working together with one mind and purpose"—and help move them from the Before column to the After column?

Because we're all in this together, I'll "Walk It Out" by

____

____

____

____

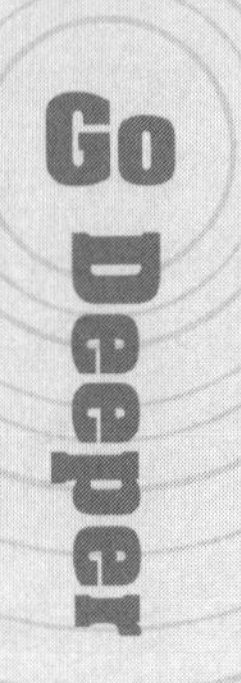

To dig deeper into how to build a team—and enjoy building it—here are some great resources:

Make Your Group Grow: Simple Stuff That Really Works by Josh Hunt (Group)

Doing Church as a Team: The Miracle of Teamwork and How It Transforms Churches by Wayne Cordeiro (Regal)

Made for a Mission by David A. Posthuma (CLC Ministries)

Church Is a Team Sport: A Championship Strategy for Doing Ministry Together by Jim Putman (Baker)

Church Unique: How Missional Leaders Cast Vision, Capture Culture, and Create Movement by Will Mancini (Wiley)

Failure Is an Option—Just Not the Final One

We now have this light shining in our hearts, but we ourselves are like fragile clay jars containing this great treasure. This makes it clear that our great power is from God, not from ourselves.

"We are pressed on every side by troubles, but we are not crushed. We are perplexed, but not driven to despair" (2 CORINTHIANS 4:7-8).

In this session, we'll journey...

from understanding that the road to success is often paved with difficulties...

to discovering that walking through those difficulties is part of the solution.

Before gathering, make sure you have...

Optional activities (choose one or both):

Come and See

- ○ **Option A:** Opening activity (see page 102)
  - ○ smooth, but not perfectly round, 1- to 2-inch rock for each group
  - ○ 6-foot-long piece of masking tape for each group*
- ○ **Option B:** DVD of *October Sky* (see page 113)

Go

- ○ **Option A:** 2 Corinthians 4:5-11 activity
- ○ **Option B:** DVD of *October Sky*, another scene (see page 113)

*See **Leader Notes,** page 153, for details.

Come and See

(about 10 minutes)

If you chose **Option A**, *read on.*
If you're doing **Option B**, *go to page 113.*

Have people get into their groups, and have groups gather behind each of the lines you've laid out. Give a rock to the person at the front of each group.

"The will of God may lie very deeply concealed beneath a great number of available possibilities.... The voice of the heart is not to be confused with the will of God."
—*Dietrich Bonhoeffer,* Ethics

» **You have one goal—to roll your rock straight down your line so it lands as close as possible to the end of the line. You'll each get one try to reach your goal. Once everyone has had a chance, take five minutes in your groups to discuss the questions for this section. Let the person who's holding the rock lead your discussion.**

Bring everyone together after five minutes to share highlights and insights from the discussion time.

"Before any great achievement, some measure of depression is very usual."
—Charles Spurgeon, "The Minister's Fainting Fits"

» **So far this season, we've focused on how to develop and share a God-given vision and how to stay focused on the great things God wants to do through us and those with us. We're now going to shift the focus for a few sessions and talk about the tough stuff. Because once this all gets real, things don't follow the plans we had in our heads. Things go wrong, or at least *look* wrong. Even when we've done our best, we might begin to wonder if we've disobeyed God somehow. Or we might feel like we've done everything right but failed God anyway. In fact, there might well be a point in time—if not a long stretch of it—where we'll stop and ask yet again, "God, was that *really* you?"**

◎ How close did you get to your goal? What would have helped you do better?

◎ Think about your last answer. Did you put the blame more on your circumstances or on yourself? Why?

◎ How do you usually respond when things don't go the way you think they should? Give up, try harder, grin and bear it, blame others, blame God? Explain your answer.

It's *always* OK to ask God that question. We need to keep talking with God, *especially* when we don't understand. But once God answers yes, it's our job to keep walking, even if we're not sure where God's leading us. Even if things aren't going the way we planned. Even when we think we're not good enough to do what God's called us to do. God knows better. He called us to this. God's plan is always better than ours, and we need to trust God so we can discover more about what *his* plan is.

We've already stepped out in faith. That's why we're here today. Now, we start learning how to keep walking, even when we have trouble seeing the details of God's plan. So let's discover how to keep walking and why it's worth it.

Seek and Find

(about 35 minutes)

> *I have discovered that it is so much harder than you think to create something out of nothing. Things happen that you never imagined would happen to you.... [Y]our own foibles [are] so much more real, more deeply ingrained and more obvious to others than you ever knew.*
>
> —Ruth Haley Barton, Strengthening the Soul of Your Leadership

» **Our case study for today comes from the life of Jacob, whom God changed into Israel. And that transformation was something only God could bring about. You're probably familiar with much of his story, but I hope this session will shed some new light on it. On your own time, read Genesis 25–50 in that new light to find out what else God might want to show you through Jacob's life. As a bonus, you'll also read about his son Joseph, whose own vision from God didn't exactly go according to plan either.**

For now, we'll look at a few key passages, and gather some insight into how God changed Jacob into Israel and fulfilled his much bigger plan by doing so. Then we'll look at what changes God might have to make in us and our plans—and maybe already has. So let's start with Genesis 28:10-22. Can I have a volunteer to read?

Let's jump more than 20 years into Jacob's future. To give a brief summary of what has happened, Jacob ran away to uncle Laban's, fell in love with Laban's daughter Rachel, and agreed to work seven years for her hand in marriage. He was tricked by Laban on his wedding night into marrying Rachel's older sister Leah; worked another seven years for Rachel, and then worked *another* seven years, during which time his wages were changed 10 times (presumably not for the better), before he finally escaped with his family and all the blessings he had tricked Laban out of.

And now, Jacob's about to meet his brother Esau—the same brother he ran away from in fear for his life just prior to the passage we read. Can I have a few more volunteers to read Genesis 32:1-12, 21-32; and 33:1-9?

Genesis 28:10-22

◎ What does God promise Jacob here? How would you have reacted to all this?

◎ Look at verses 16-17 and 20-22 again. How could Jacob's fear and amazement of the night before have changed so quickly into "If you do this, this, and this, God, then I'll do this for you"?

◎ How are we guilty of trying to negotiate God's blessings with him, especially when we're in over our heads? Is it always wrong? Why or why not?

Genesis 32:1-12, 21-32; 33:1-9

◎ What different responses does Jacob have to his circumstances?

◎ What do those responses reveal about Jacob? about God? about us?

Seek and Find continued

» **Jacob wrestled with "the Man," who obviously had better things in mind for the man who became Israel. Clearly, though, Jacob still had difficulty believing that. Maybe you're in the same situation right now. More than anything, what you need to know is that God is *still* in this vision.**

> *We know just how much we can stand, but alas, we have not discovered how much Christ can stand....To be carried through by Christ is to be left wondering afterwards how it happened!*
>
> —*Watchman Nee,* Changed Into His Likeness

Turn back to your groups. (Pause.)

Whether we've reached this point yet or not, we always need to remember which parts of this vision are truly God's, so we can keep trusting him even when we can't understand why things are going the way they are.

Several sessions ago, we gave ourselves a reality check to determine whether this was really a God thing or not. So let's step back and give ourselves another reality check. We're going to look at the same questions we answered in Session 2, but from the perspective we have now. No peeking—answer the questions in the box on top based on where you stand *right now*.

Then, just as you did the first time, come up with one action point—one thing you're going to do in response to what God's showing you *now*—and write it in your Walk It Out section. That's right—we're doing Walk It Out a little early today.

Once you've worked through those two pieces, discuss the questions at the bottom of the page with your group. Also be sure to discuss your plans to "Walk It Out" this week with your fellow group members.

Let's plan to come back together in 20 minutes.

Bring everyone back together after 20 minutes.

Ask yourself:

- As I pursue this vision, am I sensing God revealing more about the things he truly cares about?
- Will this vision, once it's realized, reveal more about God to others, or will it just reveal more about *me*?
- Which parts of this vision were clearly *not* my idea (even if I'm excited about the idea now)?
- Have I tried letting go of this idea, only to find God bringing it up again?
- Would I still want this to happen even if someone else did it—or even if I did it and someone else got the credit?

Write your thoughts about the above questions here:

Seek and Find continued

***Now*, go back and read what you wrote in Session 2.**

◎ What's changed about this vision so far? What's changed about you?

◎ As specifically as you can share, what have you been wrestling with as this vision has unfolded?

◎ What do you need to hear from God right now, to be reminded that this is still God's idea?

Walk It Out

How does what you learned today apply to where you're at right now? How can you put it into practice? Write one thing you'll do this week to make today's lesson more real in your own life. Share your choices with your group, and make plans to connect before the next session to check in and encourage one another.

Because God's still in this, whether I understand it or not, I'll "Walk It Out" by

Go

(about 20 minutes)

> *Above all the graces and gifts of the Holy Spirit which Christ gives to His friends is that of conquering oneself and willingly enduring sufferings, insults, humiliations, and hardships for the love of Christ.*
>
> *—The Little Flowers of St. Francis*

» **Jacob had an incredible vision of God's plan for his life. But he also saw a *lot* of failure and frustration before that plan was fulfilled. Again, read Jacob's full story on your own time. Take the time to appreciate what God did in Jacob's life and the far-reaching results of that.**

Let's jump ahead another 40-plus years and look at how God fulfilled his promises to Jacob—and fulfilled the promise he *saw* in Jacob.

Ask for volunteers to read Genesis 47:7-10; 48:2-4; and 49:28–50:9.

» **Think about this: One moment Jacob's years are "short" and "hard"; the next he's talking about God's blessings; and then he's passing those blessings on to his sons—the nations God promised him. Think also about the first scene here: Jacob walked in, blessed the most powerful man in the world at that time, and then *just left*.**

If you chose **Option A**, *read on.*
If you're doing **Option B**, *go to page 114.*

» **We've covered a lot of ground in this session, and there's always more to go. We never see the whole picture. We want to. We think it would be easier. We think that if we controlled the circumstances, things would be better. But God shows us what he needs to show us, when he needs to show it to us. We're blessed when we have visions like Jacob's ladder, but we're also blessed when God allows us to go through things that are painful but which enable us to become the blessings he wants us to be to others.**

Genesis 47:7-10; 48:2-4; 49:28–50:9

◎ If the Jacob of our earlier passages had met Pharaoh, what do you think would have happened?

◎ What point of your strength do you think God may be trying to break, so God can use you to truly be a blessing to others?

Ask for a volunteer to read 2 Corinthians 4:5-11.

» **Let's take a minute to silently reflect on these verses—especially if you're already in that place where you're asking God, "Why is this happening? Why *this* way? Why *me*?" Let's remember that *anyone* doing anything useful for God isn't qualified for the job. If we were, we wouldn't need, or make room for, God. So right now let's give God some room to work. Shut your eyes and reflect for a minute, and I'll close us in prayer afterward.**

After a minute of silent reflection, close your group in prayer.

Go continued

prayer ›› **Lord, thank you for stretching us and challenging us so we can become the blessings you want us to be. We acknowledge that we're often our own biggest enemies, even when we're sincerely following you. Get us out of our own way. Help us become the people you want us to be, so we can not only overcome the problems and failures we experience, but also experience your joy on the other side of those struggles. In Jesus' name, amen.**

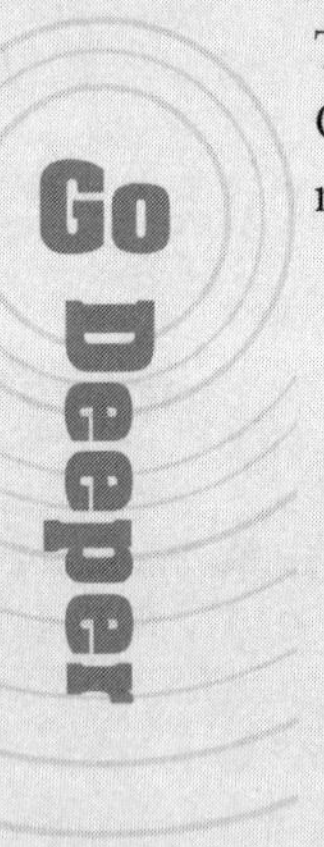

To dig deeper into what it takes to hang on to God when things get tough, here are some great resources:

Second Guessing God: Hanging on When You Can't See His Plan by Brian Jones (Standard)

Faith and Doubt by John Ortberg (Zondervan)

Trusting God: Even When Life Hurts by Jerry Bridges (NavPress)

Leadership and Self-Deception: Getting Out of the Box by the Arbinger Institute (Berrett-Koehler)

SEEING IT DIFFERENTLY

Come and See–Option B

LEADER Instead of the rock activity, watch a scene from the movie *October Sky.* A group of boys from a West Virginia mining town, inspired by the October 1957 launching of the Soviet sputnik, are attempting to create a rocket for themselves. Cue the movie to 34:53 (DVD Chapter 6), as Quentin says, "The angle of 30 degrees, crucial…" Stop the clip at 38:47, after Miss Riley says, "Now go launch yourself a rocket."

GROUP

◎ What connection do you see between the boys' failures and the adjustments they make?

◎ How do you usually respond when your plans don't go…well, *as planned*? Do you give up, try harder, slog through it, turn negative, blame others, blame God? Explain your answer.

Pick up at the leader statement on page 102, beginning, **"So far this season, we've focused on how to develop and share a God-given vision…"**

SEEING IT DIFFERENTLY

Go–Option B

LEADER Instead of the reading and reflection of 2 Corinthians, watch another scene from *October Sky.* Advance the movie to 39:06 (DVD Chapter 7), as Homer asks his brother Jim, "Couldn't you find something better to do?" Stop the clip at 41:10, after Homer tells Miss Riley, "I think we got a chance."

» **Think about the first scene we watched. Think about Homer's brother and everyone else watching. Think about what's going through the boys' heads just before the launch.**

GROUP

◎ How does success tend to erase all the fears and concerns we have, once we're on the other side of a challenge?

◎ What help do you need right now in "keeping your eyes on the prize"?

Pick up at the closing prayer, on page 112.

Patience, My Dear

In view of all this, make every effort to respond to God's promises. Supplement your faith with a generous provision of moral excellence, and moral excellence with knowledge, and knowledge with self-control, and self-control with patient endurance, and patient endurance with godliness, and godliness with brotherly affection, and brotherly affection with love for everyone.

"The more you grow like this, the more productive and useful you will be in your knowledge of our Lord Jesus Christ" (2 PETER 1:5-8).

In this session, we'll journey...

from → **to**

understanding that God's timing is God's timing for a reason...

learning how you and your team can celebrate small victories even as you wait.

Before gathering, make sure you have...

○ white board or blackboard*

*See **Leader Notes**, page 154, for details.

Come and See

(about 15 minutes)

Follow the directions in your Leader Notes. After the time of silence, move on to the discussions.

» **Get into your groups, and then take five minutes to discuss these questions:**

After five minutes, get everyone's attention, keeping people with their groups. Ask for volunteers to share highlights and insights from their discussion time.

» **In our last session, we took time to remember that God is still in the mission he's put us on, even when we run into adversity or failure. Today we're going to look at another kind of difficulty, which for some people might be even harder to deal with.**

And that's...*nothing*. We know what God wants to do, but right now everything just seems kind of dead. *We* might even feel kind of dead. But remember, it took time for God to grow his vision within us, so it's also going to take time to see that vision grow outwardly.

Making God's vision real takes a lot of work—in fact, it probably takes a lot more time than we "signed on" for. It might take awhile to see any kind of momentum, and even longer to see actual fruits from all our labor. But along the way, good things do happen. And when they do, we need to recognize them. We need to not downplay or dismiss them simply because they're not what we hoped for, but celebrate them. It's the little victories that will keep you and your team going while you wait for the big victories God has in store. So let's learn how to recognize those moments and become more mindful and intentional about celebrating them when we see them.

◎ What's your reaction to the way we started our session? What were you thinking about or feeling during that time?

◎ What's the longest you've ever waited for something? How did you handle the wait? What did you learn from it?

Seek and Find

(about 20 minutes)

> *When we aren't engaged in mission as a community, we tend toward scrutiny, because we have nothing better to do.*
>
> *—Brian Sanders,* Life After Church: God's Call to Disillusioned Christians

» Last week we looked at how God got Jacob where he wanted him, despite Jacob's best attempts to sabotage himself. In this session, we're going to look at a more classic example of patience—Jacob's grandpa, Abraham. Not that Abraham didn't sometimes get in the way of God's plan through his own impatience. Let's spend some time breaking Abraham's story down in our groups.

Take turns reading the passages listed on your group page, and then take 10 minutes to discuss the questions.

> *O Lord God, when thou givest to thy servants to endeavour any great matter, grant us also to know that it is not the beginning, but the continuing of the same until it be thoroughly finished, which yieldeth the true glory.*
>
> *—Sir Francis Drake*

Come back together after 10 minutes to share highlights and insights from the discussion time. Then discuss these questions:

 **Genesis 15:1-6; 16:1-6; 20:1-7; 20:14–21:3**

◎ What mistakes did Abraham make while (or instead of) trusting and waiting on God?

◎ What things did Abraham do right? How did those things help fulfill God's plans for Abraham?

◎ Which examples did you find yourself more focused on—the mistakes or the successes? Why?

◎ What right now has got you wondering, "Why hasn't this happened yet?" If your impatience were to get the better of you, what would your Ishmael look like?

◎ What small successes could you focus on, while you wait for "this" to happen?

Go

(about 25 minutes)

> *When someone does something good, applaud! You will make two people happy.*
>
> *—Samuel Goldwyn*

» **Turn back to your groups.** (Pause.) **Let's spend some time remembering God's faithfulness to us long before this vision was ever conceived. Take turns sharing about a time God showed up just in time—not your idea of "in time," but God's.**

After each person shares, take a few moments as a group to celebrate how God worked in that situation. Compliment each other. Clink coffee cups. Give a high five or a hug. But visibly express your appreciation for what God has done in the person's life and how God has grown him or her through that experience.

When you're done sharing, read 2 Peter 1:3-8, and take 15 minutes to discuss these questions:

After 15 minutes, ask for everyone's attention, but ask people to stay with their groups. Share highlights and insights from the discussion time, and then have groups go on to Walk It Out (or finish the Extra Impact idea on page 154 in your Leader Notes first).

Walk It Out

Get back into your groups. Let someone who hasn't led yet lead this piece.

How does what you learned today apply to where you're at right now? How can you put it into practice? Take five minutes in your groups to write one thing you'll do this week to make today's lesson more real in your own life. Share your choices with your group, and make plans to connect before the next session to check in and encourage one another.

2 Peter 1:3-8

- Why *does* God's timing in fulfilling his promises usually look so different from our timeline?

- How does remembering what God has already done help us wait for what God has next for us?

- Think about the congratulations we gave each other. Why don't we do this more often for others? And how can we change that?

- What's one thing God's doing in your life or someone else's life right now that you can celebrate while you wait?

Because I can celebrate God's perfect timing even before it's completed, I'll "Walk It Out" by

____

____

____

____

____

Go continued

prayer

Come back together as a group. Spend a little more time waiting today. Start your prayer time in silence, inviting people to pray as they feel moved to speak to God. Encourage group members not to force the prayer time along, but to let the silence hang out there as needed. Wait on God together.

Then wrap up your prayer time by thanking God for his patience with you. Ask God to help group members develop that same kind of patience with each other and with the vision God has given them. And ask God to help them develop a deeper understanding that his time is the right time.

Go Deeper

To dig deeper into how to wait for God's vision to unfold—and how to recognize and celebrate the little victories in between—here are some great resources:

God Sightings: The One Year Bible (Tyndale)

God Sightings: The One Year Companion Guide (Group)

God Sightings: The One Year Small-Group Leader Guide (Group)

Sacred Waiting: Waiting on God in a World That Waits for Nothing by David Timms (Bethany House)

What Is God Waiting For? Understanding Divine Delays in Your Life by Marlinda Ireland (Regal)

Waiting: Finding Hope When God Seems Silent by Ben Patterson (InterVarsity)

You're *What?*

"Simon Peter replied, 'Lord, to whom would we go? You have the words that give eternal life. We believe, and we know you are the Holy One of God'" (JOHN 6:68-69).

In this session, we'll journey...

from → **to**

addressing the issues that arise when others leave, for good reasons or bad...

refocusing on staying faithful to what God has called *us* to.

Before gathering, make sure you have...

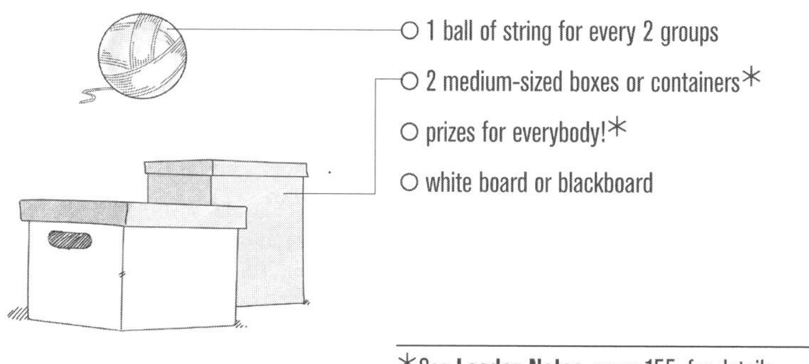

- ○ 1 ball of string for every 2 groups
- ○ 2 medium-sized boxes or containers*
- ○ prizes for everybody!*
- ○ white board or blackboard

*See **Leader Notes,** page 155, for details.

Come and See

(about 20 minutes)

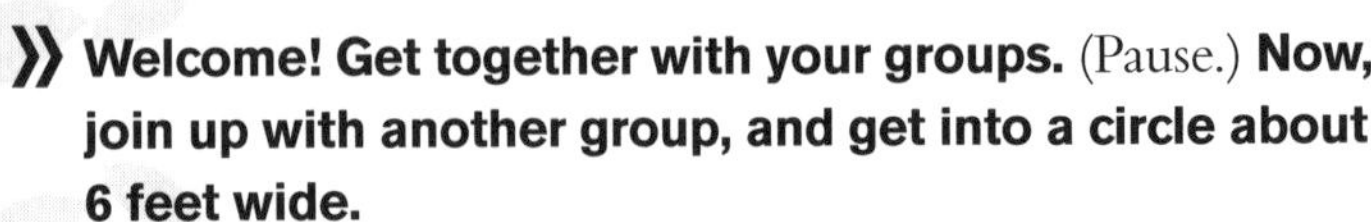

» **Welcome! Get together with your groups.** (Pause.) **Now, join up with another group, and get into a circle about 6 feet wide.**

Once larger groups have formed, give one person in each circle a ball of string.

» **Here's what you'll do: Holding on to your part of the string, toss the ball to someone else in your group. That person will hang on to the string and toss the ball to someone else, so your ball of string continues to unravel as you throw it around your circle. It's OK to catch it more than once, but make sure everyone catches your ball of string at least once. I'll let you know when to stop.**

Have groups begin to toss their balls of string around. Allow up to a minute.

» **OK, stop! Hold on to your string for now.**

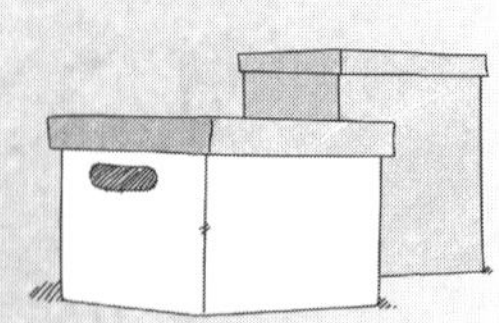

Each of you now has a choice to make—to hold on to your string or let it go. Those of you who hang on will get a prize from Box 1. Those of you who let go will get a prize from Box 2. Decide now, but don't tell anyone what your decision is. (Pause.)

At the count of three, either hang on to your string, or let it go. Ready? one…two…three!

Let those who dropped their string take their prizes from Box 2. When they're done, let those who held the string take their prizes from Box 1.

◎ What choice did you make, and why?

◎ How surprised were you by what others chose—and got—for their prizes? Why?

◎ Share about a time someone you depended on bailed at the last minute—or when you were that person to someone else. How did it affect your relationship—your connection—with that person?

» With your bigger groups, take 10 minutes to discuss our questions. The people I gave the balls of string to will lead your discussion time.

Bring everyone back together after 10 minutes. Share highlights and insights from the discussion time.

» We've talked so far about how to deal with setbacks and failures. We've also talked about how to respond when nothing much is happening at all. Now, we're going to talk about what may be the most painful issue we'll encounter as we're walking out the vision God's given us.

There will come a time when team members you've worked with and gotten close to will drop out for any number of reasons. The commitment might be too much for them or their families. They might move. God might call them to something else. They might not like the direction things are headed. And yes, they might not like the leadership, which might include *you*.

No matter why it happens—and again, it *will*—we need to remember a few things: 1) We should always want God's best for others, no matter how it affects *us*; at the same time, 2) what others decide doesn't change what God has called *us* to; and thus, 3) we need to allow God to deal with each person's decision and remain obedient to what God has called us to. So let's work through this together and learn how to deal with the issues we'll have when others leave.

Seek and Find

(about 30 minutes)

> *So stay or leave, but do both with a sense of following Jesus and loving his mission and his people.*
>
> —*Brian Sanders,* Life After Church: God's Call to Disillusioned Christians

» **Whether it's ministry or any other kind of work, turnover usually doesn't happen in isolation. It affects everyone and might raise issues you weren't even aware of. Therefore, we'll often experience aftershocks from the departure of even one person, and we'll need to deal with it as a team. Our first case study is a good example of this. Can I have volunteers to read Acts 13:4-13 and Acts 15:36-41?**

Make two columns on your white board, and label one "Paul" and the other "Barnabas." Write answers for each side. Encourage everyone to share as many ideas as possible. Then continue your discussion:

» **Fortunately, our story doesn't end there. Can I have a few more volunteers to read Colossians 4:10; 2 Timothy 4:9-16; and Philemon 1:24?**

It's easy to think of worst-case scenarios like Demas and Alexander or even Paul's painful split with Barnabas. The truth is that most of the people in our lives will be more like a John Mark or a Titus. They just move on, or in and out of our lives, for reasons that aren't personal, even though the sting we feel when they leave is still real and legitimate.

We can never know for sure what God wants to do with those he brings into, or allows to leave, our lives. The people we become closest to can nonetheless be called to other things. And when they leave, it *will* hurt, even when we're happy for them. If it doesn't hurt, we're not human. But we have to allow God to do his work in each person's life—including ours. So let's do some moving on of our own.

Acts 13:4-13; 15:36-41

◎ We can't know for sure, but what are some reasons John Mark might have chosen to leave Paul and Barnabas, based on what you just read?

◎ Based on these two passages, would you have sided with Paul or Barnabas? Why

◎ What do our two lists—and our discussion—show you about how one person's departure can affect an entire group?

◎ How can we guard against our differences becoming too big to get past?

Colossians 4:10; 2 Timothy 4:9-16; Philemon 1:24

◎ What does Paul say about John Mark in these passages? What must have changed?

◎ What other people are named in these passages, and how does Paul describe their departures?

◎ How do we keep going when others leave our team—even if they kick us on their way out?

Go

(about 20 minutes)

Ask for a volunteer to read John 6:60-70.

» **Let's face it, Jesus understands being abandoned better than anyone. This passage is just one example. Sometime later, everyone else—including Peter, despite his beautiful words here—would abandon Jesus in his time of deepest need. And yet, he chose each of them—even "a devil," whom he'd allow to keep following him until the day he betrayed him.**

Therefore, we shouldn't really be surprised by *anything* that happens to us as we choose to follow Jesus' leading. But that doesn't mean we *won't* be surprised, or upset, when others we have depended on and grown close to choose to leave, even for the best of reasons. So let's see what Jesus wants to teach us through his own experience. Turn back to your groups and discuss these questions:

Gather everyone's attention after 10 minutes, keeping people in their groups. Ask for volunteers to share from their discussion time, and then have groups go on to Walk It Out.

Walk It Out

In your groups, let someone who hasn't led yet lead this piece

How does what you learned today apply to where you're at right now? How can you put it into practice? Take five minutes in your groups to write one thing you'll do this week to make today's lesson more real in your own life. Share your choices with your group, and make plans to connect before the next session to check in and encourage one another.

John 6:60-70

◎ What different emotions and approaches do you hear in Jesus' words to Peter and the other disciples? What makes each of his responses appropriate?

◎ How does focusing on those who stick with us help us not to be overwhelmed by those who don't?

◎ How are you dealing with this issue right now—whether it's someone's recent departure or one from your past that you've never quite gotten over?

Because I'm still here, I'll "Walk It Out" by

Go continued

prayer

Come back together as a group. Thank God for the faithfulness of each person in your group. Ask God to help each of you past the hurts that come as others leave or don't follow through, whether the hurt is recent or something in the past that group members are still dealing with.

Be faithful to your group today, too. Stay around as long as it takes to pray over any unresolved issues that this session has brought up. Be there for your group, especially today.

To dig deeper into how to deal with ministry turnover of all types, here are some great resources:

Simply Strategic Volunteers: Empowering People for Ministry by Tony Morgan and Tim Stevens (Group)

Mad Church Disease: Overcoming the Burnout Epidemic by Anne Jackson (Zondervan)

Life After Church: God's Call to Disillusioned Christians by Brian Sanders (InterVarsity)

So, How Are You Doing?

"And so, dear brothers and sisters, I plead with you to give your bodies to God because of all he has done for you. Let them be a living and holy sacrifice—the kind he will find acceptable. This is truly the way to worship him. Don't copy the behavior and customs of this world, but let God transform you into a new person by changing the way you think. Then you will learn to know God's will for you, which is good and pleasing and perfect'" (ROMANS 12:1-2).

In this session, we'll journey...

from → **to**

identifying areas of our lives that are (or in danger of going) out of balance...

understanding how God wants to refill us and how to allow the Spirit to do it.

Before gathering, make sure you have...

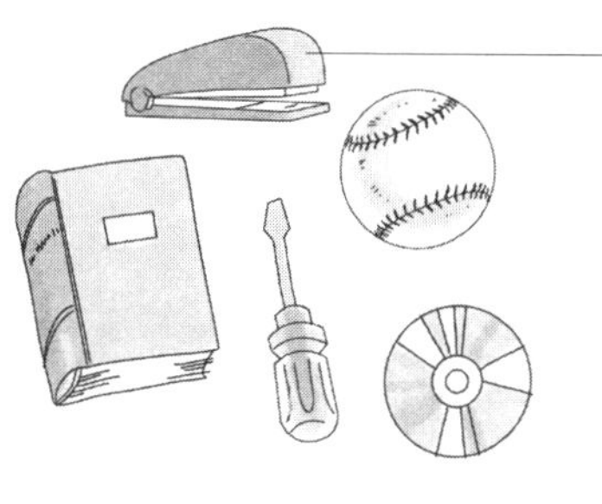

- 4 items of various shapes and sizes for every group member*

*See **Leader Notes**, page 155, for details.

Come and See

(about 10 minutes)

» **Thanks for coming back today! Everyone take four items from the table. Try to find items that have some kind of relevance to your life, and be sure to find items of different shapes and sizes. Then gather with your groups, and remain standing. I'll let you know what to do next.**

Give people time to choose their items and gather.

» **Now do the best you can to balance all your items, one on top of another, in one hand. If you drop any items, you can pick them up and try again.**

If a Christian is not willing to rise early and work late, to expend greater effort in diligent study and faithful work, that person will not change a generation. Fatigue is the price of leadership. Mediocrity is the result of never getting tired.

—J. Oswald Sanders, Spiritual Leadership

Give people up to a minute to balance their items, and then have groups sit down together to discuss these questions:

Bring everyone back together after five minutes, and ask for volunteers to share insights and highlights from the discussion time.

» **We've spent the last few weeks looking at various challenges we'll face in walking out what God has shown us and our reactions to those challenges. But even when we don't run into major issues, we can still find ourselves running on empty just from the work itself. And that's going to affect how well we live out God's call on our lives—and God's call is on every area of our lives.**

If we're truly engaged in God's work, then we constantly need God's strength and wisdom in order to fulfill that work. So today we're going to work on becoming more proactive in pursuing God, so we're relying on him when new challenges hit.

◎ Why did you choose the items you did?

◎ What would you have chosen if someone else hadn't taken it first? How did others' choices end up affecting your ability to balance your own items?

◎ How is this like the way our choices—and the choices others make—affect our ability to keep our lives in balance?

Seek and Find

(about 30 minutes)

> [T]hose who are looking to us for spiritual sustenance need us first and foremost to be spiritual seekers ourselves. They need us to keep searching for the bread of life that feeds our own souls so that we can guide them to places of sustenance for their own souls.
>
> —Ruth Haley Barton, Strengthening the Soul of Your Leadership

Ask for several volunteers to read 1 Kings 18:36–19:18. Then discuss the questions:

» **We may feel, as Elijah did, that we've done everything God asked. Like Elijah, we might even have seen great victories. Nonetheless, getting those things done takes something out of us, and suddenly we find ourselves incapable of dealing with the next challenge. Even if others might be able to look at us and say, "What's your problem? Look at how *well* you're doing!" we may still feel the way Elijah did—alone, abandoned, like no one else understands what we're dealing with. Even when God's clearly with us. And God is always *with* us.**

So let's step back and explore how we can remain in, rediscover, reconnect with, and be renewed by God's presence and power and where we might need that most right now.

 **1 Kings 18:36–19:18**

◎ How would you explain the dramatic shift(s) in Elijah's behavior here?

◎ What does God provide Elijah with throughout the course of this passage? Name as many as you can.

◎ When have you "hit the wall" the way Elijah did here? If God had asked you at that time, "What are you doing here?" (1 Kings 19:9), how would you have answered?

◎ How did God restore you? What did God teach you from that experience?

Go

(about 20 minutes)

» **Return to your groups.** (Pause.) **Read Romans 12:1-2, and discuss the questions together. When you're done, discuss how you're going "Walk It Out" this week. Then take the time to pray for each other. When you're done praying, you're free to leave** [or hang out, if you're in a small-group setting].

Gather everyone's attention after 10 minutes, keeping people in their groups. Ask for volunteers to share from their discussion time, and then have groups go on to Walk It Out.

Walk It Out

Let someone who hasn't led yet lead this piece.

How does what you learned today apply to where you are right now? How can you put it into practice? Take five minutes in your groups to write one thing you'll do this week to make today's lesson more real in your own life. Share your choices with your group, and make plans to connect before the next session to check in and encourage one another.

Romans 12:1-2

◎ When do you find it easier to try harder, or "copy the behavior and customs of this world," to get things done, than to be "a living and holy sacrifice"?

◎ What would "God's will for you, which is good and pleasing and perfect" look like in those situations? (And if your answer is "I don't know," what do you need to change in your thinking to find out?)

◎ Where do you find yourself overextended or in danger of being over-extended in your ministry or your personal life right now? How can that situation be transformed so it's fully in God's hands rather than yours?

◎ How can you invite God to continue to transform and renew the way you think in those areas so the solutions are not "quick fixes" but new ways of doing things from now on?

Because God wants to renew me every day, I'll "Walk It Out" by

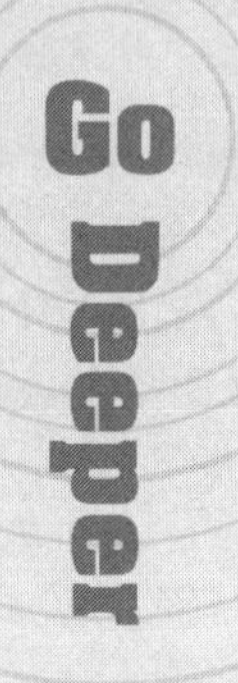

To dig deeper into how to let God transform our lives even further, here are some great resources:

Leading on Empty: Refilling Your Tank and Renewing Your Passion by Wayne Cordeiro (Bethany House)

The Good and Beautiful God: Falling in Love With the God Jesus Knows by James Bryan Smith (InterVarsity)

Margin: Restoring Emotional, Physical, Financial, and Time Reserves to Overloaded Lives by Richard A. Swenson (NavPress)

Strengthening the Soul of Your Leadership: Seeking God in the Crucible of Ministry by Ruth Haley Barton (InterVarsity)

Spirit of the Disciplines: Understanding How God Changes Lives by Dallas Willard (HarperOne)

The Meaning of Success

"So all of us who have had that veil removed can see and reflect the glory of the Lord. And the Lord—who is the Spirit—makes us more and more like him as we are changed into his glorious image" (2 CORINTHIANS 3:18).

In this session, we'll journey...

from exploring how we *can* glorify God in everything we do...

to giving God the credit for everything God will fulfill—through us and throughout eternity.

Before gathering, make sure you have...

- ○ plan for worship*
- ○ plans for a celebration*

Optional activities (choose one or both):

Seek and Find

- ○ **Option A:** Closing discussion (see page 142)
- ○ **Option B:** DVD of *Field of Dreams* (see page 145)*

DVD

* See **Leader Notes,** page 156, for details.

Come and See

(about 10 minutes)

> *To 'grow in grace' means to utilize more and more grace to live by, until everything we do is assisted by grace.... The greatest saints are not those who need less grace, but those who consume the most grace, who indeed are most in need of grace—those who are saturated by grace in every dimension of their being. Grace to them is like breath.*
>
> —Dallas Willard, Renovation of the Heart

» Congratulations! We've used an entire season to explore what it means, and what it takes, to pursue a God-given vision. And I hope all of you have gained a deeper understanding of how God's working in your lives to accomplish that vision.

But this isn't the end of our journey. It's really only the beginning. So let's start this final session by dreaming even beyond where God has already taken us. And so we can truly be ready for that dream to become real, let's get grounded, too. Let's start this dream session by considering the kind of people God dreams about us becoming, even now on earth. In your groups, take 10 minutes to discuss these questions:

Bring people together after 10 minutes, keeping them with their groups. Share highlights and insights from the discussion time.

» We've spent a lot of time exploring how to "do" the vision God has placed before each of us. But the vision started with us *being* people God was willing to take a chance on, by *being* available for God to work through us. Anything good God accomplishes through us starts and ends *with* God, and therefore any glory that comes from it is his, too. Let's take time now to *be* in God's Word and discover more about him, so we can hand all the glory over to God, where it belongs.

◎ Who's the finest person you know? What makes him or her so special?

◎ Think about the second question again. Why do his or her qualities resonate so deeply with you? What does God say to you through that person's life?

Seek and Find

(about 25 minutes)

> *If you want to figure out your path in life, you can't have an end date on the exploration.*
>
> *—John Wood*

›› In your groups, read these passages together. Read them *slowly*. Pause between readings. Take time as a group, and as individuals, to hear what God's saying through these passages *to you*. Then take 15 minutes to discuss these questions:

- Psalm 92:1-5, 12-15
- Ephesians 1:9-11
- Philippians 3:10-14
- 1 John 2:28–3:3
- 2 Corinthians 3:7-13, 16-18
- Philippians 2:12-13
- Hebrews 13:6-7, 14-16
- Revelation 4:1-11

Bring everyone back together after 15 minutes.

> *Missions is not the ultimate goal of the church. Worship is...When this age is over, and the countless millions of the redeemed fall on their faces before the throne of God, missions will be no more. It is a temporary necessity. But worship abides forever.*
>
> *—John Piper,* Let the Nations Be Glad!

If you chose **Option A**, *read on.*
If you're doing **Option B**, *go to page 145.*

›› As we finish this season—on paper, at least—and prepare for what God has in store for us next, let's take a few more minutes to reflect and share together as a group.

Psalm 92:1-5, 12-15; 2 Corinthians 3:7-13, 16-18; Ephesians 1:9-11; Philippians 2:12-13; 3:10-14; Hebrews 13:6-7, 14-16; 1 John 2:28–3:3; Revelation 4:1-11

◎ Which of these passages speaks the loudest to you right now? Why?

◎ How easy is it for you to accept the idea that you're created for God's pleasure—and that *God* delights in growing you even further?

◎ Think again about these passages and the people in your lives you shared about earlier. How can we experience God's pleasure more and more?

◎ How have you already experienced God's pleasure through his vision, maybe in ways you couldn't have imagined a few months earlier?

◎ There's really only one question left: What do you think *might* be next? Share as best as you can.

Go

(as long as you want)

Life in concert with God—ultimately that is what we are practicing for.

—*Robert Gelinas,* Finding the Groove: Composing a Jazz-Shaped Faith

» **Let's get in a circle together to close this season in a time of worship.**

Lead your group in song, however you've worked it out beforehand. (If you haven't worked it out, go to the Leader Notes *now.*)

» **Let's continue to open our mouths and glorify God for everything he's done and for everything he has yet to do but *will.* I'll start us off in prayer. As you think of things you haven't fully acknowledged God's hand in, hand them over to him. Say them out loud, and be thankful for what he's given you to share.**

prayer

Start the prayer, and then be sure group members have the time they need to pray. Wrap up your prayer time, and your season, by offering a benediction for your group. Say something like,

» **May you fully realize who God has created you to be, and become those people.**

May you reveal God's Spirit to everyone who sees your life.

May the love of Jesus spread from you to everyone you know—and beyond.

May God use you to transform and renew your world, as he has transformed and renewed you.

May your joy in Jesus be so great that nothing can contain it, so that it flows over everyone God puts in your path.

And to God be all the glory. Amen.

We know. Give us courage to trust what we know and to obey what we hope. We know that the old, old story—in our telling—becomes a new, dangerous, transforming song. And so we sing!

—*Walter Brueggemann,* Prayers for a Privileged People

SEEING IT DIFFERENTLY

Seek and Find–Option B

LEADER Instead of the closing discussion in Seek and Find, watch one more scene from *Field of Dreams.* Cue the movie to 1:30:05 (DVD Chapter 32), as Shoeless Joe says, "We're gonna call it a day. See you tomorrow." Stop the clip at 1:41:17, as the movie fades to black.

GROUP

- As you finish this season—and prepare for the next season God has in store for you—who in this scene do you most feel like right now? Why?
- Think about Shoeless Joe's comment, "No, Ray, it was *you.*" How has God already touched *you* through this vision in ways you couldn't have imagined a few months earlier?
- There's really only one question left: What do you think *might* be next?

Pick up with Go.

To dig deeper into God's definition of success, here are some great resources:

Changed Into His Likeness by Watchman Nee (CLC Ministries)

Created to Be God's Friend: How God Shapes Those He Loves by Henry Blackaby (Thomas Nelson)

The Imitation of Christ by Thomas à Kempis (various publishers)

Instruments in the Redeemer's Hands: People in Need of Change Helping People in Need of Change by Paul David Tripp (P & R)

Desiring God: Meditations of a Christian Hedonist by John Piper (Multnomah)

General Tips

- **Read ahead.** Although these sessions are designed to require minimum preparation, read each one ahead of time. Highlight the questions you feel are especially important for your group to spend time on.
- **Preview DVD clips.**
- **Enlist others.** Don't be afraid to ask for volunteers. Who knows? They may want to commit to a role such as teaching a session or bringing snacks once they've tried it. However, give people the option to say, "No, thanks" as well.
- **Be prompt.** Always start on time. If you do this from the beginning, you'll avoid the tendency of group members to arrive later and later as the season goes on.
- **Gather supplies.** Make sure to have the supplies for each session on hand. (All supplies are listed on the opening page of each session.) Feel free to ask other people to help furnish supplies. This will give them even more ownership of the session.
- **Discuss child care.** If you're leading a small group, discuss how to handle child care—not only because it can be a sensitive subject, but also because discussing options will give your group an opportunity to work together *as* a group.
- **Pray anytime.** Be ready and willing to pray at times other than the closing time. Start each session with prayer—let everyone know they're getting "down to business." Be open to other times when prayer is appropriate, such as when someone answers a question and ends up expressing pain or grief over a situation he or she's currently struggling with. Don't save it for the end—stop and pray right there and then.
- **Let others talk.** Try not to have the first or last word on every question (or even most of them). Give everyone

an opportunity to participate. At the same time, don't put anyone on the spot—remind people that they can pass on any questions they're not comfortable answering.

- **Stay on track.** There are suggested time limits for each section. Encourage good discussion, but don't be afraid to "rope 'em back in."
- **Hold people accountable.** Don't let your group off the hook with the assignments in the Walk It Out section—this is when group members apply in a personal way what they've learned. Encourage group members to follow through on their assignments.
- **Pray.** Finally, research has shown that the single most important thing a leader can do for a group is to spend time in prayer for group members. So why not take a minute and pray for your group right now?

Session 1

- Read the General Leader Tips starting on page 147, if you haven't already.
- If this is the first time you're meeting as a group, take a few minutes before your session to lay down some ground rules. Here are three simple ones:
  1. Don't say anything that will embarrass anyone or violate someone's trust.
  2. Likewise, anything shared in the group *stays* in the group, unless the person sharing it says otherwise.
  3. No one has to answer a question he or she is uncomfortable answering.
- For this season, I'm suggesting getting into subgroups of four or five. This size is a bit less intimate than in most seasons of Growing Out, but there's a reason for that. Bringing a God-given vision to life requires working with a *lot* of different types of people, and it's not always as warm and personal as we might like it to be. But it *can* be. A slightly larger group size will help you to really play with the ideas in this study, while keeping things reasonably "safe" and keeping everyone involved. You'll be creating teams who'll learn to work together for this entire season, and by doing so you'll help each other to grow. And don't be surprised if some great friendships grow out of it, too!
- In this session and the ones to come, we ask group members to take turns leading. That's intentional. Everyone's getting an opportunity to lead. Don't allow participants to fall back on a "he/she's our leader/we're the followers" mentality. Even if groups have a clear leader, use the opportunities we provide to allow God to grow each person in leadership, as people learn and serve together.

  If you're adventurous, extend this principle to the leadership of your sessions as well. Ask a different person to facilitate the session each week. Take advantage of this safer environment to get everyone better prepared for the risks they'll be taking "out there."

- If you do the second *Wizard of Oz* discussion, push for specific answers to the question, "What 'ruby slippers' will you need to keep on your feet as your journey forward?" For example, "Faith" is an insufficient answer. Push back and ask something like, "What does faith look like for *you* in your situation?" Don't ride anyone, but encourage people to articulate what they're really thinking and feeling. When that happens, *everyone* benefits.

Session 2

- If new people join the group this session, use part of the Come and See time to ask them to introduce themselves to the group, and have the group pass around their books to record contact information (page 18). Give a brief summary of the points covered in Session 1.
- By the way, if you don't already own a copy of the movie *Field of Dreams*, you might want to go out and buy one. You'll have two more opportunities to use it this season, so buying the DVD might actually be cheaper than renting it three times. Besides, it's a great movie, and it's not only about baseball—just in case the fact that it's used three times in a study about God-given vision hadn't given that away.

Session 3

- Are you praying for your group members regularly? It's the most important thing a leader can do for his or her group. Take some time now to pray for your group, if you haven't already.

Session 4

- Now that you're a month into this season, you may find it helpful to make some notes right after the session to help you evaluate how things are going. Ask yourself, Did everyone participate? and Is there anyone I need to make a special effort to follow up with before the next lesson?
- For the closing prayer time, you'll ask group members to get out their own keys. Have extra keys on hand for those who don't have keys readily available, so everyone has a key. If possible, suggest that people you gave keys to should take them home as a reminder to act on what God has shown them during this session.

  Also have a prayer request of your own ready to say out loud at the designated time if you need to help get things started.

Session 5

- Remember the importance of starting and ending on time, and remind your group of it, too, if you need to.
- For the activity in Seek and Find, you'll want rocks that are small enough for group members to hold in their hands, but large enough that they're at least a little heavy. Tailor the size and weight to your group as needed. Make sure your containers are large enough and strong enough to hold each group's rocks. Before people arrive, set out the buckets and rocks on a table or other easily accessible area.

Session 6

- For the activity in Come and See, find puzzles with no more than two dozen pieces. Make sure pieces are mixed up, so groups can't immediately see what the final result will look like. If beginner puzzles are hard to come by, you could cut a full-page magazine ad or photo into roughly 20 different-sized pieces. Better yet, use old pieces of cloth with some detail on them; it will help reinforce the point you'll explore later in Luke 5. If you use cloth, let group members take pieces home as reminders to take the vision God's given them and help others put the pieces together.

- Yep, it's another scene from *Field of Dreams*. You were warned. And this won't be the last time; you'll get the opportunity to view the scene right after this in your final session. So keep that DVD where you can find it. Also, this is a longer scene than usual. Enjoy it together.
- This would be a good time to remind group members of the importance of following through on the weekly challenge each of them has committed to in Walk It Out.

Session 7

- Congratulations! You're halfway through this study. It's time for a checkup: How's the group going? What's worked well so far? What might you consider changing as you approach the remaining sessions?

Session 8

- Set up your seats in a circle today, if you don't already do so. And if you *don't* normally do this, think about doing it for future sessions. It's a great way to get people interacting, which will result in much richer discussions. And you want everyone engaged. Remember: You're *all* part of a bigger team.
- The specific choice of snack isn't critical, but make sure you have something everyone can enjoy (multiple snacks, if necessary). You might even dress up the room and create a party atmosphere.

- If you have a small group, do the opening activity together rather than pairing off. Likewise, during the opening activity in Seek and Find, let group members do a second round with each other if there's time; let them discover more than one thing they have in common with each person.
- Before people arrive, put a sheet of butcher paper, poster board, or even several pieces of regular-size paper taped together on a long flat wall. You'll use this for the closing Seek and Find activity. The important thing is that your sheet is large enough that everyone can draw on it. Make three columns on your sheet—one narrow column in the middle (where you'll record ideas your group shares during Seek and Find) and larger columns on the left and right. Write "Before" at the top of the left column and "After" at the top of the right column. Put markers somewhere nearby so group members will have easy access to them during Go.
- Think about ways you can display the Before and After poster after this session. Hang it up each time your group meets, or display it somewhere in church with a humorous sign saying something like, "Here's what our adults made in their group today." Have fun with it, but use your artwork as a reminder that they're all part of "the big picture."
- During your prayer time, let the silence hang out there for about 30 seconds after you've read from Philippians 2. Give people time to reflect before closing your time together.

Session 9

- Do the Come and See activity on a floor that will allow rocks to roll, at least a little, and that will not be damaged by the rolling rocks or the occasional dropped rock. Use masking tape to make a 6-foot line for each group. Put the masking-tape lines at least 3 feet apart so groups have more room to work. If you're in a small meeting area, combine your groups as needed for the activity.

- Check out the options for Go. You have two very different endings to choose from, depending on whether a) your group members are already beginning to hit the wall vision-wise and really need to step back and be reminded that God's still in this, or b) they could use a good pep talk (using the second *October Sky* clip). By now, you probably have a feel for where your group's at.
- On that note, this might well be the session to remember that if you need to spend more time than just one week on a given lesson—and you're not tied to a calendar and *can* spend some extra time—then *do it*! Taking the time to understand what God wants to tell your class, group, or accountability partner(s) is *way* more important than "covering the material."

Session 10

- Before everyone arrives, write the following on your white board, blackboard, or a piece of poster paper, large enough so everyone will read it as soon as they enter:

  Find your seats.

  In a few minutes, we'll begin our study.

  While you wait, please sit quietly. Don't talk or gesture to anyone else. Just use the time to prepare yourself.

  Thanks.

  Allow five minutes before breaking the silence and beginning your discussion time.
- **Extra Impact:** Try this idea to get your group thinking about the value of divine delayed gratification. Set up a fondue pot or Crock-Pot with chocolate, but keep it covered and out of view if possible. Before your meeting time, ask group members to bring snacks that would work for dipping (without telling them why)—pretzels, cookies, brownie chunks, whatever else you can think of. If you're meeting earlier in the day, substitute cheese for chocolate,

and have group members bring bread, crackers, chips, or whatever else would work.

You'll need to add this note to the white board message you prepared before the meeting time:

Enjoy a very small sample from the snacks you've brought today as you wait. Leave plenty for later on.

After your discussion of 2 Peter in Go, bring out your fondue pot and whatever you'll use for dipping. Say something like, "You're two-thirds of the way through this season, so let's have a small celebration right now. You've waited long enough to enjoy a larger portion of these snacks, so dip as much as you'd like. Then get back in your groups and go on to Walk It Out."

Session 11

- Here's the catch in the Come and See activity: It doesn't matter what kind of prize you put in the boxes—candy, pens, temporary tattoos, whatever—as long as it's the same for everyone, in both boxes. Have more than enough prizes in each box—you don't know what group members will choose, after all. Put your two boxes where everyone can see them, but make sure no one can see inside them.
- Now would be a good time to do another group checkup—especially if you're planning on doing another study together after this. Ask yourself (and the group, phrased differently, if it makes sense to do so), "Is everyone participating?" and "Is there anyone I need to make a special effort to follow up with?"

Session 12

- Since your next lesson will be your group's last one in this book, you'll probably want to start discussing with the group what to do after you've completed this study. "Pull over" and study another subject in more depth? Will you break up and head to different groups? Make your plans now.

- For your activity in Come and See, have a variety of items available, of diverse shapes and sizes—no smaller than a marker but no bigger than a Bible. As people try to balance items, they are likely to drop them, so choose items that won't break easily. Be creative in your choices, as your items could also be used during your discussion time afterward. For example, a fork might lead to someone sharing about spending too much time and money eating out; a stapler could start a discussion about workaholism; or a small building block might suggest a need to spend more time with family. Put all your items on a table before your meeting time.

Session 13

- Since this is your group's last session in this book, make sure you have a plan for next week...and beyond.
- If you use the clip from *Field of Dreams* during Seek and Find, build in at least 10 extra minutes. Adjust the time for Go as needed; I've built in some extra room so you can do that easily.
- For your closing worship time in Go, look for a member of your group who has a musical gift, and ask him or her use it and lead everyone in song. If you don't have a musical talent among your ranks, find a good worship CD to play and sing along. Whether or not your group includes someone who can be a worship leader, be sure to spend time worshipping in song today. Take as long as you need to cultivate a spirit of worship among your group. And take joy in God's presence as you do!

  As you invite people to pray, be sure to have in mind something for which you want and need to give God glory. You might need to get your group started. (You could acknowledge God's hand in the lives of your group members this season.)

- Have some meaningful fun at the beginning of this session. As people enter, play some music that's appropriate to the occasion—the "Hallelujah Chorus," "Ode to Joy," or even a graduation march. You could even serve up some graduation cake. Help your group celebrate that God *has* been doing something special in their lives this season—and has even more in store for them.
- Plan to do something special after your session, too, or plan a separate celebration for another time and place. It's your call.

No matter what you do, congratulations! You've made it through this season—and through Growing Out (although your *real* growing out is just beginning…)! It's my hope, and my prayer, that God has blessed your entire group as you've walked together these past few months—and that you'll continue to let God lead all of you forward together.